P9-DDY-908

While the Christian ministry is primarily a vocation, its successful prosecution depends on proper technical equipment. High ideals call for high standards in presentation. The aim of The Minister's Professional Library is to supply the modern minister with a series of authoritative books covering the professional side of his work: the actual techniques of worship, preaching, the pastoral office, running the physical plant of the church. It will present and exemplify those high professional standards which are as necessary in the ministry today as they are in medicine or law. It will include only books addressed directly to the minister in his professional capacity. It is essentially a working library which will, in time, cover the whole field of ministerial activity.

THE MINISTER'S JOB

The Minister's Professional Library

THE USE OF THE BIBLE IN PREACHING
By Carl S. Patton

PLAIN THOUGHTS ON WORSHIP
By Edwin A. Goldsworthy

THE BUSINESS ADMINISTRATION OF A CHURCH
By Robert Cashman

THE MINISTER'S JOB
By Albert W. Palmer

THE PREPARATION AND DELIVERY OF SERMONS
By Carl S. Patton

FORM AND FREEDOM IN WORSHIP
By Clarence Seidenspinner

Other volumes to follow

THE
MINISTER'S JOB

BY

ALBERT W. PALMER

President, The Chicago Theological Seminary

WILLETT, CLARK & COMPANY

CHICAGO   NEW YORK

CONTENTS

CONTENTS

THE MINISTER'S JOB

Wide was his parish, scattered far asunder,
Yet none did he neglect, in rain, or thunder.
Sorrow and sickness won his kindly care;
With staff in hand he traveled everywhere.
This good example to his sheep he brought,
That first he wrought, and afterwards he taught. . . .

To draw his flock to heaven with noble heart,
By good example was his holy art.
No less did he rebuke the obstinate,
Whether they were of high or low estate.
For pomp and worldly show he did not care,
No morbid conscience made his rule severe.
The love of Christ and his apostles twelve
He taught, but first he followed it himself.

— Chaucer, Leonard's Translation

INTRODUCTION

THE MINISTRY holds new appeal for the youth of today. It is an old vocation with a modern meaning. How old it is Chaucer's picture of the ideal parson in his day clearly reveals. Chaucer died in 1400. There is something reassuringly permanent and stable about a calling whose professional standards and ideals had crystallized on so high a level more than five hundred years ago.

And yet the minister's task is also perennially new — and never more so than today. Life is ever in flux and the work of a spiritual leader is to reinterpret it on its highest levels to each new generation. He has, as it were, to teach a horse-and-buggy age how to fly an airplane and yet preserve its understanding and appreciation of old Dobbin and the one-hoss shay! It is just because life has changed so completely in a thousand ways that the ministry continues to be so indispensable and exciting a calling.

The following pages describe the minister's job today. They are not written primarily for ministers — although probably many a parson will read them, and I hope with interest, as he checks up on his own program and procedure. I have written primarily for the young man who is in the valley of decision regarding the choice of a vocation and for his counselors in courses on vocational guidance. I am persuaded that many a youth who is really fitted for the pastorate and thinks of it more wistfully than he would be willing to confess, fails to choose the ministry as a life work because he has inadequate, false or prejudiced views as to what religious work is all about. To reveal the realities of this great calling, root out prejudices and clear the road for a new generation of Christian leaders is the purpose of this book.

But, someone might ask, is there really a need for more ministers — isn't the profession overcrowded already? My answer is that no profession today is overcrowded with first-class, adequately trained men, least of all the ministry. Even during the depression the seminary with which I am connected had no trouble in placing its graduates within a few weeks after graduation. Of course the question may arise: It's easy to place eager young men right out of school — but what about the man of forty or fifty? Well, that is the critical age in every vocation, isn't it? The answer is that only the man who chose his life work wisely, who secured good training, who has kept up with the literature, thought and methods of his profession, attended its conventions, taken graduate work and adopted new and better techniques as they have come along, is secure in medicine, dentistry, law, engineering or business management. Ought he to expect any greater security in the ministry? For men who will stay alive and keep growing, serving the Christian church presents an unparalleled opportunity today. But, as I frequently say to candidates for ordination, " Plan to do your best work after you are fifty years of age." No man ought to enter the ministry unless he is determined to keep young, resilient, informed, growing and open-minded at least that long.

It may be objected that no one man can possibly be sufficiently versatile to measure up to all the requirements set forth in the following pages. No one is more painfully conscious of that fact than the author. He has had more than twenty-five years' experience in the pastorate and this book is by no means a self-portrait or a record of achievement. Will not such a portrayal of the minister's job, then, tend to discourage the neophyte and especially the young man who is examining different vocations in the attempt to find his true life work? The answer, of course, is that some temperaments will kindle to one phase of the parson's work and some to another. What I have tried to present is a fairly balanced account of the rich total possibilities of the Christian ministry today. I hope that many a young man will find them calling out to him for accomplishment, and will rejoice to choose and prepare for no shallow, superficial task but one which will challenge all he has of imagination, fortitude and good will. But if he tried to do and be all the things that this book suggests are within the range of the ministry as a vocation, he would probably die the death of the proverbial chameleon on the Scotch plaid! But I have warned him!

CHAPTER ONE

THE MINISTER AS PREACHER

PREACHING is exciting business! It always has been — ever since the days of Amos or the Franciscan friars or Martin Luther. More, it has to be, for if it isn't the congregation goes to sleep or stays home, and the preacher might better plow corn. It is exciting business because it deals with the primary interests of life and seeks to answer the great questions which arise in the human heart in every generation: What am I? Why am I here? What are the supreme values in life? What ought I to do? What are my right relations with other men? What is the universe? How is it created, upheld and guided? If I get out of harmony with life, if I feel that I have sinned, how can I find peace and poise and righteousness again? Who and what and where is God? What is my duty toward him? What might it mean to be in tune with the Infinite? What awaits me after death? — These are ever recurrent questions. Trying to answer them in terms appropriate to the knowledge and problems of each new generation makes preaching an exciting business in every age.

The preacher has his difficulties today. He has more competition than ever before in history. He has to be more versatile than the Sunday paper, more alluring than a baseball game, more interesting than the movies, better informed than the latest book, more enticing than a drugstore window filled with different brands of whisky! And he lacks some of the

4

advantages which reinforced the preachers of other days: he has no universally accepted authoritative book, no social compulsion for church attendance, no unique possession of education or of social status. And he confronts an age apparently absorbed in material comforts and mechanical gadgets — autos, radios, airplanes and a general taste for streamlined luxury. The men he addresses are pre-committed to getting rich quick and have probably been conditioned in their thinking by a prejudice against religion. They think of faith as contrary to science and of the Bible as a collection of discredited superstitions and unbelievable fish stories. Some of them regard religion as the opiate of the people and others as an impertinent social disturber and breeder of revolution. So, caught between the two, how shall the preacher present both the social gospel and the ministry of comfort?

Nevertheless, the preacher has certain advantages on his side and if he really knows his business he can meet all these difficulties and overcome them. For he deals with life at first hand. All these other things touch it at second hand, but the preacher deals directly with the human soul. For that reason religion is always and must ever be more real, more gripping, more authoritative in the lives of people than all these secondary things. There is nothing so thrilling as to get religion!

Great preaching is more than entertainment or information or even physical well-being, for it meets man himself in his inner need of satisfactory adjustment to life. The secret of its power and precedence over all other interests may be seen in the old Negro spiritual, " It's me, Lord, standin' in the need of prayer." Because humanity senses that need religion will always stand first in human concern and great preaching will never be disregarded.

Moreover, the modern preacher has certain compensations to balance his handicaps. For one thing, he has freedom of utterance. No other man is so free — not the editor, nor the politician, and certainly not the businessman, who is proverbially timid. The minister is expected to tell the truth as he sees it without fear or favor. He has no personal financial ax to grind, and men look to him for an honest appraisal of life's values. His function has also been marvelously enlarged in recent days. Once he was supposed to interpret only the Bible, but now he is expected to interpret all of life. In interpreting life he will make large use of the Bible, but he must include more; he must also interpret life in the light of history, of science and of philosophy, and add to that common sense and current literature and everyday experience! A large order? But that is what makes preaching such exciting business. And where preaching is done with honesty and fervor people will prefer it to the movies, the Sunday paper and the auto all put together!

Another thing that helps the minister today is the recovery of God as an inescapable fact and force in the world. We are passing out of the age in which God was to many people little more than an oblong blur, as the old lady once said he was to her. And we long ago left behind the age when God was just a character in the Old Testament who spoke Hebrew and lived in the neighborhood of Mount Sinai. God has become a contemporary once more. We find him in the creative order of the cosmic process as revealed by science. We find him in the all-pervasive, invisible, yet ever present wisdom and power that upholds and guides the universe. We find him in the moral law, in conscience, in the quest for beauty. Economics, sociology, psychology are only new ways of learn-

ing the order and truth at the heart of things, new insights
into the will of God. Great preaching has always been born
out of great convictions about God. No age has ever seen
God more grandly or more clearly than the best thought of
the world is seeing him today. Great preaching, on fire with
a sense of the living God, is sure to come out of this vision.

Add to this the recovery of Jesus, and you see why preaching is entering a new era of authority and power. Fifty years
ago Jesus as ordinarily presented in Sunday school was a
strange, unearthly figure, the second person of the Trinity,
walking the earth thinly disguised as the Carpenter of Naza-
reth but knowing all the time that he was God Almighty,
subject to none except self-imposed human limitations. We
no longer think of our Lord Jesus Christ in so unhistorical
and unhelpful a fashion. The Christ of the Gospels has come
back to us, thanks to modern biblical scholarship, and we see
the great Galilean as Peter and Andrew saw him. Sometimes
he almost seems to walk with us as he walked with them!
We know him as one who sat wearied by the well-curb of
human life, who wondered if faith would survive on the
earth, who prayed in agony of spirit, who was a man of sor-
rows, well acquainted with grief. But we also know him as
one who spake as never man spake, as one the beauty of whose
life and greatness of whose ideas bind our hearts to him in
deathless loyalty. We have the doctrine of the incarna-
tion back again! He is for us both human and divine, our
highest, holiest manhood and also our deepest insight into
the character of God and the possibilities of the universe. We
bring all life before the judgment seat of Christ. There
is something to preach about that can set men's souls on
fire!

Against such a background, where does the preacher of our age find themes for his sermons and how does he set about preparing them?

The best sermons grow out of the preacher's insights into the life problems round about him. He sees the struggles, sins, frustrations and discouragements of men and women in this modern world setting. But he also sees the heroism, the dogged endurance, the deeper spiritual insights, the unexpected beauty and inspiration with which life at its best may be lived. Then he goes back into the Bible, back into great literature, back into poetry and music and the beauty of nature, back into the experience of his own soul, back to Christ, and along this way he finds the answer. He has not only the Bible as written in the Old and New Testaments, inexpressibly precious as that great document of the human spirit is to him; he has also the continuing bible of the human race. St. Francis, John Bunyan, the Pilgrim Fathers, Lincoln, Kagawa, Gandhi and a hundred more are in it. All that is noblest and truest in science, art, biography, music, philosophy and poetry — all that the human race has learned or sought to know of God — is there. What a bible to preach! What a privilege and responsibility to be a preacher!

Nor does he preach just to individuals alone. He preaches to the state, to the social order, to the modern mood, to civilization, to barbarism! Jesus' idea of the kingdom of God, the conception of a social order based on justice, love and mercy, has come back to earth again. Over against war, race prejudice, economic exploitation, ruthless greed, the preacher envisions a civilization of brotherly men and a social order wherein Christlikeness can find expression. He walks with the Hebrew prophets, he shares the impulse that drove Sir Thomas More to write *Utopia* and Plato the *Republic*. No delicately perfumed little essays are delivered from his pulpit Sunday morning — he knows that " the Lord hath spoken, who can but prophesy "! The very urgency of the times, the appalling possibility of a world tragedy if peace and good will do not replace militarism and economic greed, put a thrilling note of prophetic appeal into all great preaching these days. We preach to men as in the days of Noah!

What are the marks of a good sermon?

First of all it must have a message, something with which the preacher is so on fire that he is bound to say it no matter how. The sermon may be a work of art or it may not, but it must be a work of reality. It must ring true. Its note of urgency must have no quavering.

Second, it must have variety. Some men have only one sermon and wear it threadbare. A great preacher will be like an organ with many stops, not like a piano with just one set of strings.

Third, it must have a definite theme. Better announce the topic so that the congregation will know what you are trying to talk about. Usually it is well to have a text, too. A great text puts tried and tested authority and mellow age behind the transitory human being in the pulpit.

Fourth, it needs a good introduction, brief but interesting; a problem stated with all its challenging difficulties, as Fosdick does it; or a story which carries at its heart the sermon's message, as Charles Gilkey does it; or a thrilling, arresting sentence, as Charles R. Brown sometimes does it.

The fifth thing is a logical outline. Your thoughts must

march determinedly from one point to the next. A sermon is not a merry-go-round; it must get you somewhere — you and the congregation!

Point six is imagination. It is said that art teaches us to see — it teaches us what to see and it teaches us to see more than we see! Preaching is an art, an imaginative art. Its interest depends partly on its ideas and partly on the imaginativeness with which those ideas are unfolded and illustrated.

In the seventh place, a sermon must be definite and concrete. " Don't I argufy and sputify? " asked the old Negro preacher of the committee demanding his resignation. " Yes, but you don't show wherein," was their annihilating answer. The preacher must always show wherein!

And finally, the eighth and most important point, the sermon must be profoundly and genuinely spiritual. You are not a radio announcer mechanically recommending something you never use yourself. You are to reveal your own soul and its experience with God.

And if there were a ninth point it would be brevity. You must not be too long — nor too short either! Souls have been saved after the first twenty minutes!

Does your heart thrill to this conception of preaching? Are you willing to pay the price of equipping yourself to preach in this large and vital way? Are you willing to read and think and study; to plow your way through economics, sociology, psychology, history, science, literature and art; to expose yourself to all that will quicken your human sensitivity through music, drama, nature, travel and, perhaps most of all, through human service and suffering? Then perhaps you are one who ought to be a minister.

But a minister is more than a preacher, he
is also a priest. So maybe you had better
read the next chapter before deciding.

CHAPTER TWO

THE MINISTER AS PRIEST

MANY PROTESTANTS do not like the word " priest " and the average young man would probably recoil from the idea of being one. It may be interesting to note, however, that the word comes from the same root as " presbyterian "! " Priest " is only a shortened form of the word " presbyter," which means " elder." The most Protestant of denominations and the most typically Roman Catholic of titles are both derived from the same word.

But " priest," as I am using it in this chapter, does not mean a man in a rear-entrance collar and a black suit, pledged to celibacy and empowered to perform mass. Such a man may be a priest in the meaning here set forth or he may not — it all depends. But a priest, in the large and universal meaning of the word, is any man, or woman too, who becomes a channel whereby men and women become conscious of God. The priestly function is the God-revealing function. He who ministers to human souls so as to make God real to them is a priest in this larger sense of the word.

Protestantism has its priesthood. One of its most ancient doctrines is the priesthood of all believers. This doctrine means that each soul can have immediate personal access to God and has no need for the intervention or intercession of any ecclesiastical ceremonial or official. But it also means that we can all interpret God to one another so far as we have experienced him. No truly priestly soul can ever refrain from sharing the divine fire. He is a Promethean spirit and lives to serve his fellow men. The Protestant minister is not a priest in any exclusive sense. He has no use for sacerdotalism. He is a priest only as any spiritually sensitive soul may be one. His only advantage is that he has the time, training and vocational place which give him great opportunity to use what priestly gifts he has. But ever and anon he will meet some thoughtful layman, some noble and mature personality, even some unspoiled youth, whose clear-eyed priestly insight and sensitive discernment will leave him humble and longing for greater spiritual gifts.

The minister will fulfill his priestly functions both as a pastoral counselor and as a leader of public worship. The next chapter will deal with counseling; let us devote this one to the organization and leading of worship.

In far too many Protestant churches, especially those of a nonliturgical tradition, the so-called worship service is often hardly more than a collection of " preliminary exercises " preceding the sermon and interspersed by the arrival of late-comers. People who would not think of being late for a wedding or a dinner engagement and who catch the eight-fifteen train with unfailing punctuality seem to feel that if they reach church before the sermon, or at least before the collection has been taken up, they are not unduly late.

The minister, therefore, has a primary responsibility for making the Sunday morning worship service a truly mystical experience for all who are in any degree capable of it. Here is one of his great opportunities to break down the walls of sophistry and pride, of drab routine and deadening materialism, and let the light of the divine presence shine into the hearts of those who attend his church.

How shall he set about it?

First of all, he must be himself a worshiper. He must be responsive to the divine beauty all around him in nature, in music, in art, in human life, in the Bible. And he must long with an unalterable yearning to bring his people in touch with all these riches until the hard sophisticated businessman shall go out of church on Sunday morning saying: " There is a God! I have been strangely uplifted this morning "; until the waster and the worldling, if they have been present, shall say: " That was the real thing this morning! I wish I could experience such faith and joy "; until the mourner or the frustrated and beaten-down shall say: " I can lift up my heart again! There is something undefeated at the heart of the universe that will uphold me "; until youth with its hopes and plans shall say: " That is what life means to me — God and a better world and life set to the music of great ideals! "

Much will depend upon the choir. They may sing well or not quite so well, but their skill is of secondary importance. The primary thing is that they shall be delivered from the corrosive influence of the concert psychology. Somehow the minister must bring it to pass that they do not sing to the congregation for their approval, not even to the music committee, but that they count their music an offering to God himself, " singing and making melody in their hearts unto the Lord." To that end he will need an organist or director who understands or is willing to learn about worship as well as music. Then he will do well to share with the choir in frequent brief conferences his understanding of worship and his conception of what a particular service might do for people. Under such teaching anthems and solos will lose their undue individualistic emphasis and merge into the symphony of worship. They may, indeed, often be replaced by responses, softly sung without announcement, quietly and unobtrusively leading the movement of the worship service on to its great goal.

It will also help the choir greatly if their location in the church is as inconspicuous as possible — in a rear gallery from which their music can float down in antiphonal responses, or in a chancel where they join with the congregation about the altar or communion table with its cross or open Bible or other symbol of our Christian faith. Let us hope that the day is passing when the organ, the choir and the preacher seem to be the central objects of adoration in church. Better that the congregation should gather around the Ark with its sacred Scriptures, as in the Jewish synagogue, or around an altar or communion table with its cross and lighted candles, as all denominations of Christians are coming more and more to do.

There is no time here to go into the details of a really great service of worship. It may well have a processional symbolizing the going up of the soul into the sanctuary, and the service itself should move in a great sequence which will include the vision of God, the confession of sin, the sense of cleansing, new insight into the divine beauty and a final dedication to work the will of God. It should leave the congregation hushed and receptive to the words of the preacher, whose sermon, after such a service of worship, will find itself cleansed and purified, less prone to harsh and irritating self-assertive judgments but more powerful to awaken self-criticism and real humility in all who hear.

The priestly function of the minister would be greatly helped if we had better hymnbooks in the pews or if such hymnbooks could be supplemented by books of worship materials. My ideal hymnbook would be one having well chosen hymns with such words and tunes as the congregation can sing with sincerity and joy, plus a treasury of material out of which the leader may draw what he needs for his service of worship according to the occasion. In place of the long stiff responsive readings from the Psalms, or the completely worked out worship services which must be used in their entirety or not at all, there should be Scripture passages of varying lengths chosen not only from the Psalms but from all parts of the Bible having liturgical beauty and dignity. Some may be read responsively but the shorter ones should be read in concert. Moreover, there should be selections drawn from the religious poetry of all the world and from the great storehouses of the literature of devotion and social aspiration in all the centuries. There should be confessions of faith, collects and longer prayers, litanies and other responsive prayers, and also antiphons and responses for the choir. Given such a hymnbook, the minister will be able to make his worship service much richer in spiritual beauty and emotional uplift for the worshiper.

But, after all, with or without a good hymnbook and with or without a helpful choir, it is the minister himself who will largely determine how fully the worship service fulfills its priestly function. His bearing and demeanor will have something to do with it — he must not be fidgety or trivial or self-conscious or pseudo-impressive. His very clothes may play their part — they must be appropriate; a khaki shirt and trousers may do beside a campfire but I prefer a gown in church.

But the greatest contribution the minister makes will be his prayers. The pastoral prayer is, in the Protestant service of worship, what the elevation of the host is in a Roman Catholic mass — the supreme symbolic moment of communion with the divine. Inasmuch as a living person pouring out his soul to God is a greater and nobler symbol than anything inanimate or physical, this prayer should lift the service to the highest level of aspiration, mystical power and hushed expectancy. That this is not always so, that it may be even a time of boredom and relative inattention, is the fault of the minister, due perhaps to his lack of appreciation of its significance or to his inadequate understanding of how to lead his congregation in prayer. It is better for a church service to be known for its worship than for its eloquence; and a minister, while he may feel a passing sense of satisfaction at a word of appreciation for his preaching, knows that such words are superficial indeed compared with a quiet and even faltering syllable of gratitude for the prayer.

A good pastoral prayer depends first of all on the depth and intensity of the minister's own sense of the reality of the God to whom he prays. The religious press some time ago was agitated with the question, "Can the humanist pray?" I think he can — for the present, at least. It is not the correctness of his idea about God which conditions the prayer so much as the sincerity and intensity of his conviction of the reality of the particular God to whom he prays. Better prayers may come from men tremendously in earnest about a very partial, vague and inadequate sort of God than from men of much theism but little fire. Of course, if this is so, it follows all the more that the nobler and more adequate the prayer leader's conception of God, the better; and in the end one cannot but feel that prayer will hold its deepest emotional potency only when God is supremely real and personal to him who prays. It is hard to see how a sub-personal God can continue to awaken the emotion of prayer after the language and unconscious influence of a theistic tradition have passed away. Even your humanist prays in anthropomorphic terms and personalizes his prayers.

The first step, then, in a good pastoral prayer is a spirit of hushed and devout waiting, by the minister himself, before God as the supreme Oversoul of the universe. If the minister is not in the noblest sense a priest at the moment of public prayer he only goes through a mummery and empty form.

The second step is also a priestly one in the finest, broadest meaning of the term. He who leads in prayer must gather to himself with a sympathetic and understanding heart all the varying needs of the waiting congregation. Aye, and more, for he must feel the world outside and its needs — the disinherited, the prisoner, the foreigner, the forgotten. But, particularly, he must enter with a constructive imagination into the lives of the men and women here before him. Let him say to himself: Here are the troubled, the bereaved, the wistful; here is the tired mother, the harassed businessman, the numb victim of routine; here are the lonely, the stranger and the unemployed, the injured and mistreated, the disillusioned and the superficial, the tempted, the fearful and the sinning. Even the hypocrite is here! But the minister will do well to remember that the joyful and triumphant are also present — youth with its vitality and hope, maturity with its mastery and achievement. Religion must not seem to such merely a consolation and a caring for the wounded; it must also sound a trumpet in the dawn. All the intimate knowledge and winnowed wisdom of his pastoral experience, gained in the course of his going in and out among his people or through their coming to him with their troubles, will be the background of his prayer. What a thrilling task it is for the minister thus to catch the varying moods of the congregation, gather them all together and bring them, hushed and humble and expectant, into the attitude of worship.

How shall he do it? Now the issue will depend largely upon his sense and power of emotional leadership. He is to lead not only their minds but their hearts and wills. Much will depend on the service which has just preceded. In general it is well to precede the pastoral prayer by a brief but deeply devotional responsive service designated the " Call to Prayer," followed by a verse of some old hymn sung softly by the choir, and then by a period of absolute silence before the spoken prayer begins. This silence should not be too long and it should be preceded by a definite invitation: " Let us now wait before God in silent prayer."

Something depends upon the minister's voice. It should be low but not too low, deep but not too deep, and there should be in it a warmth and vibrant quality which is sympathetic without being sentimental, honeyed or artificial. Reality, reverence, reassurance, expectancy are communicated by the voice even before the thoughts are uttered. A minister may well guard his health and deny himself rich food, late hours, cigarettes or any other dissipation if thereby he can preserve his voice as a better instrument for the worship of God.

But a voice is a vain thing unless it has something to say. And so the content of the prayer is all-important. First of all, the prayer should not contain too much. We don't need to give information to God — he knows before we tell him. The purpose of the prayer is to bring us to God, not God to us; its keynote, as Fosdick says, should be not " Give me " but

" Use me." It must deal, then, with the vital concerns of the congregation — either with the things that are keeping them apart from God or with the open doors through which they may pass into the inner sanctuary. It should never be a sort of disguised bulletin of the week's events or a concealed announcement like the famous petition devised by the college president, " O Lord, bless the French class which thou knowest will not meet at the usual hour of ten forty-five this morning! " And yet it may, and indeed often must, deal with what is in the focus of attention. For example, what minister could help praying for President Roosevelt when in those dark and somber days of March, 1933, he took over the presidency of the United States?

Is there any preferred order in public prayer? Order there should be in the leader's mind, but it may well be changed from time to time lest, to the congregation, it become routine and stereotyped. In general, the writer finds his pastoral prayer tending to arrange itself as follows: First comes the cry of the soul for the presence of God:

> O God, in whom we live and move and have our being, gather us close to thee now in the hour of morning prayer. . . . Out of the turmoil of the week, out of the dust and smoke of daily life, out of all our troubles, out of all the cheap and trivial things of the passing hour, we come, O Lord, into this sacred place and this holy hour that we may listen for thy voice and hear that only.

Sentences like these lead easily and naturally into the mood of confession. What the prayer book calls " a prayer of humble access " follows almost inevitably:

We recognize, O God, that merit lives from man to man and not from man, O Lord, to thee; and so we come with no false pride or sense of undue importance but humbly and simply, as children to a well beloved Father.

Petitions for forgiveness, new light, added strength, continued guidance, follow naturally and then the prayer lifts itself to look out on wider horizons and we pray for others — the stranger, the tempted, the bereaved, the overburdened, the ill. On it goes to yet wider concerns and interests — the church, the missionary, the city, the nation, the world. And then, before it closes, let it come back to the personal again:

O Lord, beyond these spoken prayers, each one of us brings to thee in the quiet of this holy hour his own personal, intimate, inarticulate longings and aspirations — all we could never be, all we aspired to be and were not, thoughts hardly to be packed into a narrow act, fancies that broke through language and escaped. . . . O Lord, hear these unspoken yearnings of our as yet unrealized and nobler selves as we lift them to thee in the peace and quiet of this hour, through Jesus Christ, our Lord. Amen.

And then, very softly, as though an echo far away, the organist plays a verse of some old beloved hymn against a background of distant chimes, and the prayer is done.

Of course it is quite obvious that all this requires, in the noblest, truest sense, literary skill; only it must not be a self-conscious, pretty, ornamental, flamboyant or rococo kind of literary skill. It must have at times the ruggedness of the hills and the realism of a Doric column. The language must

be that of reverence and of dignity: it is better not to call God
" you," though with uneducated men that may sometimes be
the acid test of reality; neither do men want any easy familiarity with that august and mystic Spirit which broods over
the universe, and yet there must be something which is beyond reverence and dignity — there must be intimacy. Intimacy but not familiarity! For a man must be intimate with
the God of his own soul, yet he must never be familiar.

How shall a man master the language of devotion? By
loving it and making it a part of himself. Some of this language is in the Bible — there is the fountainhead, of course.
But it is also in the prayer book and in modern books of
prayer like Joseph Fort Newton's *Altar Stairs,* McKee's *Communion with God,* Orchard's *The Temple,* Rauschenbusch's
Prayers of the Social Awakening and Stevenson's *Vailima
Prayers.* A verse or phrase from an old hymn will often lift
a prayer to a new emotional level. Finally, a man must love
and cherish poetry if he would pray. He must not use long
quotations — never that! — but faint and far-off echoes of
the great poets which will fill his prayer with overtones that
people will hear, not always knowing what they hear, with
spiritual joy and uplifted hearts.

Other things being equal, the minister's public prayers will
be impressive and uplifting in proportion as they are truly
and deeply intercessory. A man may well forget his sermon
when he begins to pray lest he preach it twice! A prayer is
not an essay or a philosophical debate. It may well be a confession of faith, however, especially as it gets under way:

> O God, we believe that beyond our wavering sense of
> right and wrong there is a justice that shall never know

defeat, and that beyond our imperfect appreciation of the beautiful there is a beauty which is eternal and un-dimmed. We reach out to the supreme goodness and cast ourselves upon the mercy that cannot fail.

All this is good. But the prayer must go on to *plead* for some-thing. It is the intercessory note that stirs the human heart. " Here is a man talking to God and asking for something that he needs and that we all need " — when the congrega-tion begin to say that to themselves they also are lifted on the wings of prayer.

The objects of intercession should be changed from week to week. Keep the prayer short; one Sunday you may plead for doctors and nurses, another Sunday for teachers, and yet another for missionaries and social workers. Pray frequently for the ill, the tempted, the troubled in mind or body or estate, the stranger. People will be grateful to you for constant re-membrance of " those we love and those who love us, wher-ever they may be," and for " the gratitude we owe to those whose devotion has been a benediction to our lives and who have brought us light and healing." Also, as Charles W. Gilkey has well said, " while you cannot preach about the social gospel every Sunday, you can pray about it! " There-fore with all your soul be an intercessor for peace, for racial and economic justice, for the city of love and beauty, for a civilization of brotherly men, for childhood.

Should the minister write his prayers and read them? Per-sonally I do not do either. We of the Protestant tradition have a great word in connection with prayer — we do not " read " prayers, we " make " them. A prayer should be *made,* it should strike the creative note! Of course there is a place for liturgical and responsive prayers, and the writing of prayers is one way of learning how to use the language of devotion. But in the supreme moment the congregation will be lifted higher by one who makes his prayer, pours out his soul to God in spontaneous adoration, than by any reading.

Perhaps a word should be added about what may be called "minor" prayers. How may a man learn how to deliver an invocation or say grace without wandering all over the lot? Here a study of the special form of prayer called the "collect" might teach the minister how to combine brevity with dignity, impressiveness and spiritual appeal. Just an ascription, a petition, a reason for the petition and a remembrance of Jesus Christ, and the prayer is done.

> Almighty God, unto whom all hearts are open, all desires known and from whom no secrets are hid, cleanse the thoughts of our minds by the inspiration of thy Holy Spirit that we may perfectly love thee and worthily magnify thy holy name, through Jesus Christ, our Lord. Amen.

What could be more perfect?

Do you see what this chapter has been getting at? What feeling have you regarding the need for worship as a contribution to the strength and comfort of men's lives? Do you sense the possibilities in being a priest as well as a preacher? Then possibly you are one who ought to choose the ministry as a vocation.

But there is more to this priestly side than just leading public worship; there is pastoral counseling. So turn to the next chapter.

CHAPTER THREE

THE MINISTER AS COUNSELOR

BETWEEN a new and more appreciative understanding of the value of the Roman Catholic confessional and the new insights into mental conflict which are coming out of the psychiatrist's consultation room, the pastoral work of the Protestant minister bids fair to be reborn. I do not look to see confessional stalls with green curtains and kneeling benches set up in Protestant churches, and I certainly do not want the minister to become a psychiatrist — he has a big enough job already. But it does seem clear that in fulfilling his priestly function as a counselor the minister has much to learn from both the confessional and the psychiatrist which, wisely used, would make him on occasion possibly an even more helpful adviser than either the padre or the practitioner. Pastoral counseling is nothing new in Protestantism. Preaching, for instance, is a kind of pastoral counseling done impersonally. It has always been understood that if the coat fits it may be put on! Of course the preacher must never say that, and part of the power of preaching has been its anonymity. The preacher is never supposed to hit at particular members of his congregation. If he is wise and considerate he will observe this principle to the letter. But, nevertheless, faithful preaching will carry good advice and searching counsel home, and not infrequently to places where they are desperately needed although no one outside suspects the need.

Worship may also sometimes prove to be pastoral counseling at its highest potentiality. It may be far more effective to pray in church for a forgiving spirit than to tell a man on the street his duty of forgiveness. To pray for the homes of your parish may go far deeper into the needs of some particular home represented in church that morning than could any pastoral advice.

The Protestant minister also has a great advantage in that he is traditionally expected to make pastoral calls throughout his parish, as the Catholic priest is not. And he has an advantage over the psychiatrist in that he does not have to be paid for services to the soul or wait to be called before rendering them. As a pastor he can tactfully offer his services where the situation needs them. These two advantages work together. By his pastoral calling he learns inside facts about the home, family and business life of his parishioners which are important in helping him to be a wise counselor. Viewed in this light, pastoral calling ceases to be a mere perfunctory ringing of doorbells and becomes a most valuable opportunity for acquiring wisdom and understanding and often for rendering spiritual first aid.

Moreover, pastoral calls are not the only contacts which the minister has with individuals. If he is a good pastor he meets his men, where he is welcome to do so, in the round of their day's work or on the golf course. He sees people in committees and at all sorts of social functions. In all these contacts his attitude is always one of good will and friendship. If he is psychologically wise and knows what to look for and what to listen for, he may learn much that will help him be of service later on.

The good pastor's relationship to his people differs in still another important respect from that of either the priest or the psychiatrist. It is much more informal. The minister carries his confessional and his consultation room around with him — even though he may and ought to have office hours at his church for people who want to lay their troubles before him. But some of his best leads and greatest opportunities will come quite casually along the way. It was that way with Jesus, wasn't it? But they will come only if, like Jesus, the minister knows what is in man and appreciates his opportunity to speak the ministering word.

How, then, does a minister become a wise pastoral counselor? First of all by study. Seminaries now offer courses in mental hygiene, personality disorders and pastoral counseling from a psychiatric point of view. And if he has never had such courses, or even if he has had them, good books are constantly appearing which the minister can read. But, as Robert Louis Stevenson once remarked, "literature is a mighty bloodless substitute for life," and so he who would be a counselor must know much about the real lives that people live.

Travel is another way of coming to know life because in a different environment we become alert to things which are taken for granted at home. But, though a trip to Europe or Japan is worth all it costs and more, travel need not be long and expensive, for there are stay-at-home journeys which are almost equally educational.

Did you ever, for example, see the inside of the jail in your town, ever spend a day in a mental hospital, ever visit the juvenile court? Did you ever stay over night in a perfectly respectable cheap hotel like one of the Mills hotels in New

York City? Did you ever hunt for a job, ever work in a print-ing office, drive a delivery wagon, cross the ocean on a trans-port, preach in a leper settlement, sleep with a bunch of sol-diers in an army camp, act as a " super " on the stage, travel two thousand miles in a freight car, earn your living as a can-vasser? Ministers have done all these things and more in their relatively sheltered lives, not as a preparation for coun-seling but just in the line of duty. And they have thereby gained sympathies and insights which have helped mightily when it came to dealing with men and women in the pastoral relationship.

The first preparation for pastoral counseling, then, is to know the theory of it — the best books and courses on mental hygiene and psychological insight; and the second prepara-tion, which must go right along with the first, is to know life — the rough-and-tumble sea of its realities and not just its protected coves and placid harbors.

But there is a third preparation, if the counseling is to be *pastoral* counseling, and that is to know religion!

If you are going to be a good pastoral counselor you must hammer out a theology and a practical philosophy of life. You will need to have some working conception of God, some idea of the significance of personality and of man's place in the universe, some basic ethical convictions and a fairly clear conception of the character of Jesus. If to these you can add a faith in the eternal life and its abiding values, a vital experience with prayer and a knowledge of the Bible, you'll have a very helpful background for your task.

What kind of problems come up in the pastoral counselor's experience? All kinds! At least all that people think he might possibly help them with. It depends largely on what kind of man he is, what he preaches about on Sunday, how realistic he is in dealing with questions tentatively raised in conversation with him. Some ministers will have relatively little pastoral counseling to do. Their sermons are so remote from life and their bearing so austere, or so frivolous, that people would never dream of inviting them into the inner sanctuary of their lives. They would rather tell their troubles to the policeman.

But the pastor whose sermons reveal experience with life, a humble spirit and an understanding heart, from whom people feel they can reasonably expect sympathetic help in analyzing their problems and not just denunciation or ex-communication — such a pastor will find all the varied problems of life brought to his door. Some of them will be absurdly simple and foolish, others so difficult that he can only pray for light to deal with them, for he will find no solution without God's help.

The catalogue will include difficulties growing out of adolescent tensions, parents' misunderstandings of their growing children, children's need of insight into the baffling ways of worried adults. Problems of sex ignorance or mis-information or emotional reaction. Problems of family ad-justments — homes headed for the rocks because of disregard of the basic principles of complete financial, intellectual, sexual and emotional cooperation in marriage. Problems of business ethics, of economic disaster, of poverty, destitu-tion and relief. Problems of vocational guidance and unem-ployment. Problems of quarrels, suspicions and long cher-ished feuds. Problems of advancing age and its fears, of loneliness, of helplessness. Problems of divorce and hasty marriages and of people who have never been married. Problems of sickness, invalidism, death. Problems of drink, insanity and crime.

What can the minister do when all these things are brought to him for counsel and solution?

Well, first of all, he can listen! What most people need, or at least desire, is an audience. Remembering that people are supposed to listen to him on Sunday, he can return the compliment by listening to them during the week. This is a large part of the technique of the psychiatrist. If people can only express themselves fully and completely to someone they trust, the very release of getting all their troubles out of their system will sometimes clear up the difficulty. Having said all they have to say, they may at last be able to analyze their own problem, with perhaps the help of a few hints from the outside. If they think they have solved their problem themselves, so much the better.

In the second place, the wise pastoral counselor will learn not only to listen but what to listen for. He will come to detect certain overtones or undertones which will reveal to him things he needs to know. Here is a woman, for example, who praises her husband with such eloquence and so ubiquitously that all the men in the parish wish their wives, too, had been gifted with similar insight and expressiveness. But a wise observer notes that she talks too much about her husband. She does, and there's a reason. Six months later they are divorced!

Here is a man who comes to you with a perfectly plausible story. At least it seems so at first. But as you talk with him you find that he makes no concessions to any difficulties you point out, but, on the contrary, has an answer to everything all thought out in advance. You can make absolutely no impression upon his utterly relentless logic. Mere facts mean nothing to him. At last you realize he is either a high-pressure salesman or the victim of a fixed idea, headed for paranoia — or already there.

After he has listened, what can the pastoral counselor do? He can talk things over in the light of such psychological wisdom as he has been able to acquire, plus practical common sense and ordinary Christian ethics and good will. It will be best to draw out the counselee on the question of what these common-sense Christian principles should be in this particular case. What, does it seem to him, would be the fair, generous, gracious, cooperative solution? What would be the first step toward it? How can that step be taken?

Sometimes the problem seems insoluble. Both pastor and consultant, after pooling all their knowledge, are still baffled. What then? Well, perhaps there is other wisdom that can be drawn upon. Maybe this case requires more expert analysis and advice. Let's talk it over with a trained social worker, or a wise woman — perhaps the minister's wife — or a lawyer, or a doctor, or a psychiatrist. Then too, time solves many problems. Sometimes all that can be done is to wait. But since the consultation has taken place, the troubled soul does not have to wait alone. One can wait so much more patiently if his anxiety is shared and he knows that his pastor waits with him.

Two things the pastoral counselor must never do: he must never be shocked and he must never betray a confidence. He must never be shocked because all reciprocity stops the moment his voice or expression registers shock. Or possibly it was the hope and intention of the person telling the story to shock him; then he must not permit such easy satisfaction.

In any case, in reacting negatively the minister blocks the way to any common ground of realistic approach toward the solution of the problem.

There is an old story of a man who had committed murder and who, overtaken by remorse, felt an impulse toward confession. Being in front of a church he found his way to the pastor's study and burst in crying, " I have committed murder! " The pastor replied: " Wait a minute. I must speak to my secretary," and stepped into the adjoining room. " Miss Smith, call the police! I have a murderer in my office! " When he returned the man was gone. Wandering down the street, the murderer came to a Catholic church and thought he would try again. Within he saw a priest just entering the confessional. Hastily he knelt before the little grating: " Father," he whispered, " I have committed murder! " Clear and cool and undisturbed came back a friendly voice: " How many times, my son? "

As to betraying a confidence, that would not often happen deliberately. The peril of betrayal lies in the nature of the minister's job. As a preacher he is always on the search for apt and vivid illustrations. The temptation to use what has been told him in confidence in order to drive home the point of a sermon is sometimes almost irresistible. " It occurred so long ago, or in another parish, or it can be disguised by changing the names," he says to himself. But he should never forget that gossip travels across the miles and across the years. Moreover, the very fact that he used a confidence as an illustration may be just the thing that will keep away from him some sensitive and troubled soul. " I wouldn't want my case to be exploited that way," she says and keeps her problem to herself. The fact that courts have ruled that a minister is not obliged, any more than a priest, to reveal what is told him as a pastoral counselor ought to impose upon the pastor a special responsibility to be very reticent about the use he makes of such material. Such reticence will be rewarded by the increasing trust and confidence of his parishioners.

Finally, the pastoral counselor must never forget that his is a priestly function, that his supreme service is to bring the troubled soul into harmony with God. Other adjustments may be made along the way but they are only partial and preparatory. The truly adjusted life is adjusted to God. This does not mean that the minister should flood his caller with pious talk. He may not mention God at all at first and may even seem to avoid conventional religious phrases and procedures. His patient may be conditioned against such language, or, more pathetic still, may accept it too easily. But insofar as he brings his patient into touch with reality, into harmony with truth and love and forgiveness, he is putting him in tune with those qualities which are at the heart of any real God. He may have first to reconstruct the patient's whole theology without the patient's realizing it, dropping the conventional language of religion for the time being. But in the end his work will not be complete until adjustment, conscious and accepted, has been made to God, to Jesus and the Bible, and to the church. The altar fires of prayer and worship will once more be kindled within the sanctuary.

———✧———

But the minister doesn't spend all his time counseling. He has an organization to run. Hence the next chapter.

Chapter Four

THE MINISTER AS ADMINISTRATOR *

THE MINISTER these days rarely founds the church of which he is the pastor; he inherits it. And, like all things inherited, it has some characteristics which are inexpressibly precious, some which ought to be discarded, and yet others which must be retained but reconstructed. How to recognize these three classes of things and deal with them appropriately and effectively will test a minister's tact and good judgment.

A wise and experienced pastor once said to me: " Make no changes the first year. Devote yourself to preaching and pastoral work. When you have set their souls afire and they have come to know you and to trust you, then you can do things which would have caused a riot if they had been attempted prematurely." Sound advice and ordinarily to be followed to the letter in the case of an old and stable church. But it should also be remembered that there are unstable churches which would die on your hands if you did nothing to improve their organization the first year.

* This chapter could well be shorter than the others because so much of the ground has been admirably covered in another book in this same series, *The Business Administration of a Church*, by Robert Cashman. But the student considering his vocational choice may not have that volume available and, in any case, it represents the viewpoint of a layman. Since I am speaking as a minister there will be a different accent as well as additional material in this chapter which may possibly be of value as a sort of footnote to Mr. Cashman's excellent and practical manual.

Before he sets out to organize or reorganize his church the minister will do well to consider carefully questions like the following:

What is the denominational background and genius of this church?

What peculiarities are there in its local history and situation?

What type of people make up its constituency and with what sort of secular organizations are they accustomed to deal?

What attempts at reform were made and failed in the past and why?

What deep-seated prejudices and personality problems are involved?

Where is the strategic place to begin?

By the time he has acquired sufficient knowledge to answer these questions the pastor will probably decide that the reorganization needed is not a one-man job, that the church belongs to its members and they need to be aroused to its problems and educated and organized for their solution. To this end he may organize a planning commission to study the whole problem and bring in a report. He will, of course, give the various subcommittees through which this commission operates a lot of hunches and feed them as much good material on their particular problems as he can find or as they can digest. The commission ought to be a composite affair — some of its members being church officials, some chosen for their interest or knowledge of the questions involved. And it may also be wise to have some very conservative members, so that they may make their criticisms in advance. Being on the commission and exposed to its discussions may convert them and, in any case, will lessen the force of their opposition later on. It will be like having a member of the Supreme Court inside the President's Cabinet.

As a pattern for such an analysis of a parish, the following outline might serve. It comes largely from a form prepared by President Albert W. Beaven of the Colgate-Rochester Divinity School, with some additions from Dr. Ozora S. Davis and myself. While not a complete or scientific survey, it will help church and minister to see their parish problems in relation to one another and in perspective.

(1) What is the church's worship program? Is it really worship? Where does it fall short? Why?

(2) What is the church's teaching program? Is it real and effective? Is it Christian? Is it intelligent? Does it help the church or compete with it? Does it meet community needs? Does it reach both adults and children?

(3) What is the church's evangelistic program? Has the church any evangelistic mood? If one method is outworn or repudiated, what other method could be used? Is the church really propagating the Christian religion?

(4) What are the church's community relationships? Does it do anything for the community? Is it an isolated club or an instrument for service? Is it of any use during the week? A map of the parish, locating all other churches and social agencies, would help here.

(5) What is the church's Kingdom vision? Has it information and vital relations to Christian work abroad

or at home outside its parish? Has it an aggressive message as to war, race relations, social justice, civic welfare?

(6) Does the church have any denominational cooperation? Is it a free-lance church or does it cooperate? How?

(7) What equipment does the church own? Has it the kind of tools needed to work with? If not, why not? Laziness? Lack of vision? Lack of money? Is it well located for its task?

(8) What is the state of the church regarding finances and what stewardship ideas and methods may be built up? What about its credit and business standing? Are the community resources being fully cultivated? Debt? Plans for its payment?

(9) What is the tone of the church's spiritual life? Is it a secularized church? What are its spiritual ideals? How expressed?

(10) What social life does the church have? Is it an instrument of fellowship? Or is it cold?

(11) What are the church's special problems? Ebb tide of population? Change of racial makeup? Economic changes? Extreme poverty? Extreme wealth and frivolity? Isolation? Competition of other institutions? Overchurched community? Past record of quarrels or scandals? Is it a "one-man church"? Other problems not listed?

(12) What should the future policy be? Broad outlines of the best strategy for future development and service (a) for one year, (b) for five years.

Out of the report of such a planning commission, and out of the educational discussions and debates which it will arouse, there should finally emerge a policy, a program and an organizational pattern adapted to your church and to its local situation. The report will be expressed not only in words but in charts and diagrams. Duties, responsibilities and goals will be clearly allocated and officers, committees, boards appointed, departments organized.

What then? Well, then all that remains is for the minister to be a good executive and keep the plan working. That is not so easy. It involves several things, among them these:

(1) The minister must see to it that each officer, committee or department is adequately informed as to its area of responsibility and the work expected. Definite training may be necessary.

(2) Provision must be made for regular reports from time to time, either at church meetings or in the church calendar or parish paper. People work toward definite goals, not for vague general aims. They must have an opportunity to see and tell what has been done.

(3) Due recognition and generous but not fulsome praise must be given. This is the only recompense an unpaid volunteer staff receives apart from the individual's own inner satisfaction at having shared in a good work.

(4) There must be rotation in office, not too frequent but not too long delayed either, so that new leadership can constantly be developed.

(5) The plan itself must likewise be kept growing and flexible, to meet the changing needs of the parish. A

small carefully selected committee may be charged with this responsibility alone.

(6) The minister may well keep himself in the background as much as possible. He should train the church to operate on its own. Besides, his time and energy need to be concentrated on preaching and counseling.

I shall not attempt to outline any particular plan of church organization, for such a plan will depend largely on the denominational pattern and this is a book for all denominations. But let me now pass to what is often the critical point in the success or failure of church or any other kind of administration: the art of dealing with difficult individuals.

The sociologist tells us that people work for four great motives — security, recognition, mastery or a sense of craftsmanship, and adventure or new experiences. Where any or all of these are frustrated there is bound to be friction and unhappiness. When industrial management discovers these motives and takes them seriously a new day will dawn in labor relations. But, meanwhile, a new day might dawn in many a church if these four objectives were posted directly over the minister's desk and ultimately registered in his understanding. Except for its relatively small employed staff the church has little to do with people's security, but the minister who understands his parishioners' need for the other three satisfactions of life can go far toward making a happy church. Give people a chance to do something well, open avenues of exploration and new experience for them, give ample recognition to their personalities and contributions to the total program, and your church *esprit de corps* will flourish.

And if trouble and antagonism do arise, the wise executive, after reviewing these four motives and finding nothing amiss, will try to analyze the difficulty further. Is this friction due to a misunderstanding of facts, or to a misapprehension of motives? These errors can be cleared up by frank and gracious conference. Or is the friction due to an honest difference of philosophy and values? This deacon thinks cooperatives are a purely economic matter, for example, while the parson feels that they may be a valuable experiment station on the way toward a less selfish social order. Well, here again there can be frank and honest conference with mutual respect and courteous recognition of the other's viewpoint. The motto of a famous Christian conference in China was, " Agreed to differ but resolved to love "; that is a basic Christian attitude, but we must beware lest it get twisted around into, " Agreed to love but resolved to differ."

Two words of warning may be useful here. The first is, never question motives! You can keep contact with a man and you may ultimately win him so long as you do not question his motives or even his rationalization of them. Give him a chance to save his face! And the other warning is one I learned from one of Chicago's outstanding business executives: " Concerning pleasant things, write; concerning difficult things, confer." In other words, if you have to discharge the organist, don't write her a snippy little note. Be brave enough to talk it over with her. Let her feel in your tone of voice the genuine kindness of heart which no letter can convey. She may be angry and say some unpleasant things but you must see to it that her ultimate memory is of a man who was courageous enough to talk things out, who maintained his composure, and whose every word and tone conveyed nothing but good will.

And this perhaps suggests one other warning, and that is that many people are quite deficient in sense of humor. I may be misled by the quality of my own jokes, but my observation is that a minister can never depend on it that his jokes will be understood. Especially is this true of irony, which should be indulged in sparingly. As for sarcasm, that is reserved for the heroes and villains of the screen; it is not for ministers! Of course a minister must have a sense of humor, otherwise he would die, but it must be like the humor in McCutcheon's cartoons, without sting or bitterness.

Does some minister or prospective minister say: " I am willing to preach and pray and counsel. But deliver me from this administrative job, I can't be chained down to that! " Yes, but do you realize that it is precisely on the administrative side of his work that the minister comes nearest to sharing the life and experiences of his laymen? They have to deal constantly with problems of organization and routine. They have to learn how to get along with all sorts of people. Who are you to preach to them on Sunday if you are not capable of bearing efficiently and cheerfully the same kind of burdens and irritations they bear all week long?

Perhaps this is a good place to turn to a more appealing side of the minister's work and consider him as a teacher.

Chapter Five

THE MINISTER AS TEACHER

JESUS was frequently addressed as " Teacher." The man who would be a Christian minister may well learn, therefore, all he can of the teacher's art. I say this in spite of the fact that the epistle of James says, " Be not many of you teachers! "

The teacher's technique requires knowledge of both the subject and the person to be taught. It involves patience, slow but steady progress toward distant goals, and great resourcefulness in awakening interest in the unknown, arousing latent abilities, and stimulating an imaginative and constructive attack on life. The teacher's approach is one of invincible good will and his personal attitude that of modesty and humility. He counts himself a channel through which knowledge flows rather than the sole artesian well where it originates. Now let us apply this conception of the teacher's job to the minister's and see where we come out.

First of all, the minister must understand the subject he is to teach. He must be in some sense a scholar. A later chapter will deal with the minister's educational training but it may not be amiss to indicate here that his whole life long he must keep alive and develop that scholarly approach to the problems of his profession which it is to be hoped he has acquired in the theological seminary. Happy the pastor whose church has a fund for buying books which may not be diverted to any other object. But even without this, and on a very meager salary, he will still find the seminary library ready to loan him books for the postage, and most public librarians are very generous about ordering books which ministers indicate they would like to read.

The importance of studying human nature and of understanding the people whom he would serve has already been suggested in the chapter on counseling, but a word should be said about the teacher's spirit of patience and his method of making slow, steady gains toward distant goals. A very excellent book written some years ago is *The Impatience of a Parson*. Parsons should be very impatient — but they should not show it too much! A display of impatience never gets a teacher anywhere; it is contrary to his whole plan of campaign.

Lyman Abbott never attended a seminary; he secured his early theological education in the old-fashioned way by studying with an uncle who was pastor of a rural church in Maine. Because his uncle's farm was called "Few Acres," Abbott used to refer to it as the "Few Acres Theological Seminary." In his autobiography he says that the greatest lesson he learned there was that, in order to move an object from one point to another, you must move it through all the intermediate points. Many a seminary would justify all its endowments and atone for some of its theological sins if it could be sure of convincing every student of that very elementary proposition.

It is very thrilling to be a prophet and very noble to be a martyr, and it may seem drab and commonplace to be a teacher — finding out where people are in their religious and social ideas, starting with them at that precise point, and then skillfully awakening curiosity, discontent, interest, self-criticism, vision, progress. But it should be remembered that the greatest prophets were also very resourceful teachers. Note the psychological skill of Isaiah with his yoke or of Jeremiah buying that corner lot in Anathoth. And as to martyrdom — well, to teach a stiff-necked, unresponsive generation year after year with patience and with unfailing urbanity and hopefulness may not be as picturesque as being burned at the stake, but who shall say it is not martyrdom?

What I mean is this. Any man can come into town with a line of denunciatory sermons of which every syllable is true, and get everybody by the ears in no time. At the end of three months the American Legion, the D. A. R., the Chamber of Commerce, the Ladies' Aid and even the Central Labor Council will be so incensed at him that he will have to look for another job. What has he accomplished? Added to a reputation for lack of tact, he has left a divided church and a disgruntled community and has made things twice as hard as they ought to be for his successor. And, while he is adjusting the mental halo of his self-inflicted martyrdom in some new parish, another man with the same essential convictions but with a teacher's technique can come into that community, smooth its ruffled feathers, win its confidence in his personal kindliness and good sense, touch its conscience, appeal to its human sympathies, feed it a few thousand facts in moderate quantities of from one to half a dozen per sermon, and sooner or later the community itself will say: " There is a lot in what he says. Of course we don't swallow it all. He has some pretty radical ideas, but we believe in him. And on some matters we've changed a good deal since he came. He's given us a new slant on this Council for Social Action, for instance. We used to think it was in the pay of Moscow but now we recognize its value as a safety valve. The church has got to face these problems. And, say, that last number of their little magazine did have some facts in it that make you sit up and take notice, didn't it?"

The minister's teaching program will be a many-sided one, depending on his community's situation. It will vary with the size of the church and with its location — suburb, a great city, an industrial section, a town or village or the open country. But in one or the other of these places it will employ the following teaching opportunities.

First of all, the sermon, whatever else it may be — and it should be a great deal else — will lodge as many important facts and good ideas as the congregation is capable of absorbing, and probably a few more. David Starr Jordan once told me his objection to most preachers was that if they had two ideas they used one and saved the other for next time. The preacher should not be economical with his ideas. But at the same time one irritating idea is about all a single sermon can carry. It is better to balance it with several others easier to assimilate. The worship service, in which the sermon is embedded, is also in part, but only in part, a teaching function. We certainly learn about some things, and open the door to learn a great deal more about them, by praying for them. As Charles Clayton Morrison has so vividly brought out in his book, *The Social Gospel and the Christian Cultus,* the implications of the religion of Jesus for social action will not really grip the conscience until we have woven them into the liturgy of our worship.

Another valuable teaching opportunity is in the Sunday

evening or weekday forum. An outsider who does not have to live in the community, if he knows his facts and is an interesting speaker, can often say provocative and challenging things, and answer both sincere and nasty questions in a way that will forward the cause of clear thinking in the community. One of the most strategic moves the church can make in these days of threatening totalitarianism, whether communist or fascist, is to build up a tradition of free speech. No real or searching education is possible without it, except possibly in the field of pure mathematics.

Other teaching opportunities will be found in the midweek meeting and in the adult Bible classes. Many a women's society, also, could be quite transformed and vitalized by an adequate teaching program concerning missions, Bible study, personal religion, child guidance or civic welfare. Moreover, the minister has frequent opportunities to address Rotary clubs, high schools, colleges, women's clubs and all sorts of conventions. On such occasions he has his choice between giving deft and skillful entertainment and starting some really educational thoughtfulness in his audience. " Many's the lecture I'se listened to and wondered whether I'se been receivin' education or entertainment," says Uncle Eph. Well, the minister ought not to leave his audience in too great doubt. Even the opportunity to give a book review may serve his turn. If there were no ideas in the book, why not suggest a few that ought to have been in it?

All the foregoing has to do primarily with the education of adults. But the great field for teaching is with young people, and this educational companionship with youth is one of the minister's greatest privileges. There is the Sunday school to start with. Does it really teach the Bible and make it glow with interest and contemporary meaning? Read Halford Luccock's *Preaching Values in the Newer Translations of the Bible* or Carl Patton's *Use of the Bible in Preaching* and you will see what may be done to make the Bible a living book. If the minister does not teach the Bible or get it taught so that it kindles enthusiasm and appreciation, no one else is likely to do so, and the race will lose some very great literature and, incidentally, a lot of very important ethics and religion. "You can't be near that man without learning something about the Bible," is not a bad recommendation even for a modern minister. If the devil shouldn't have all the good tunes it is still more true that the fundamentalists shouldn't have any monopoly on the Bible. Their theories prevent their making any good use of large parts of it anyway.

But the minister must see to it that his Sunday school is far more than a Bible school. It must be a school of life where youth confronts real situations and sees them in the light of sound ethical ideals against the background of human experience as revealed in great biography, drama and philosophy. The teaching need not be all literary either. Social exploration trips will make these problems still more vivid and unforgettable. Religious drama may well be given an important place in this educational process, and, beyond what we ordinarily call drama, that which is the highest drama of all, namely, worship. For in a rich and well conducted worship service the individual soul lives through that most dramatic of all inner experiences, the coming into right relations with the universe and into harmony with God. Share a well prepared and impressively conducted candle-lighting service with a group of young people and you'll learn more about worship than you teach.

And then, on the mundane side again, there is the scout troop or the summer camp where the minister who is a good swimmer or a good woodsman or a good banjo player — almost any accomplishment will do — can live with youth, and enter into its thoughts, and prepare to say something intelligible and even gripping to the rising generation later on. Meanwhile what he is may have spoken more deeply than anything he will ever have the chance to say.

And this is a good point from which to pass on to the next chapter and consider the minister as a human being.

CHAPTER SIX

THE MINISTER AS A HUMAN BEING

MUCH MORE of normal human liberty is allowed the minister today than was customary in days gone by. In some parts of the country the minister may even smoke and dance, and nowhere is he any longer required to wear a Prince Albert coat and a white bow tie. Personally I neither smoke nor dance, but I do appreciate being delivered from the long-tailed coat and the white lawn tie. Perhaps the best advice as to his personal behavior and appearance ever given to a young minister was this: "When you go to a new community, do not dress or behave in such a way that everyone will immediately spot you as a minister. But on the other hand, don't dress or behave in such a way that they will be shocked when they learn that you are one!"

Shall the minister wear a clerical collar and a high-cut vest? The answer depends largely on personal taste, the custom of his denomination and section of the country, and the practice of his fellow ministers. Most men will prefer not to be conspicuous and for that reason may choose to dress in quiet good taste like other men. Dressing so, they feel that they see and hear life as it really is. The wind of masculine profanity and outspoken opinion is not tempered to the shorn lamb of professional dignity as it would too often be if the minister dressed so that all men recognized his calling at once. On the other hand, my friends who wear clerical garb tell me that in making calls, visiting a hospital or even taking a long railway journey, they find that people turn to them more readily.

Should the minister wear a gown in the pulpit? By all means, if the architecture of the church is not too incongruous with such a costume and if the choir is also gowned. There is a curious prejudice and inconsistency widely prevalent which allows a robed choir without dissent but feels that if the minister were likewise vested it would indicate that he, and maybe the whole church, was headed straight for Rome. As a matter of fact the black Geneva gown is the most Protestant of garments. John Calvin wore one. Need any more be said?

What shall the minister be called? I know ministers who are called by their first names throughout the parish, and this informality is an expression of affection. But generally the minister will prefer to be just plain " Mr. Smith." The undertakers in the north and everybody down south will probably call him " Doctor." That is the chief argument for a theological student's getting a Ph.D. while in college — it will save him lifelong embarrassment in handing back " doctorates " or feeling that he ought to. But whatever else he is called, he should never be called a " Reverend." That is a widely prevalent barbarism which all friends of good English should suppress. " Reverend " is always an adjective and never a noun. The proper form is " the Reverend John Smith " or " the Reverend Mr. Smith " — never just " Reverend Smith." One can no more say " Reverend Smith " than he can say " good Smith." One has to say " good John Smith " or " the good Mr. Smith." Protestants need an adequate title for their ministers corresponding to the Catholic's

" Father " and the Jew's " Rabbi." The Lutherans use " Pastor," which serves admirably. I wish the rest of us could do likewise or else revive the good old English title of " Parson " before we all become " Reverends " willy-nilly.

But there are more important human problems before the minister than what he shall wear or by what name he shall be called. There is the problem of his business affairs. He ought to be " an utterly honest man," as a Japanese student once quaintly told me in an examination paper. That includes paying his bills and not issuing rubber checks. If he needs money he had better take the chairman of his board of trustees into his confidence and arrange to borrow on a businesslike basis rather than ruin his credit and the credit of the church by unpaid bills. His best form of saving will be life insurance plus membership in the pension fund of his denomination. He has no business going into business. Preaching is the only business for him to follow and it will require all his brains and energy. He must also beware of the commercial enterprise that may want to exploit his name and standing. They are not for sale.

Certain minor problems of morals arise in the minister's life. Shall he play cards? It's a terrible waste of time, except perhaps on a six weeks' voyage around Cape Horn. But whatever he plays, he will not gamble — no Irish sweepstakes for him! Shall he smoke? I always advise against it, but must admit my advice is largely disregarded. Some of our greatest preachers have been and are smokers. Shall the minister go to the theater? How out of date that question has become with the universal presence of the movies! Shall he dance? His problems will be fewer if he does not. Shall he drink? That he simply cannot do and retain his standing

in the community — and he will not want to if he has read
Haven W. Emerson's *Alcohol and Man*. Moreover, as his
pastoral experience widens and he sees what alcohol does to
youth, to family life, to some of the finest people in the world,
he will turn his glass down with emphasis and without the
slightest longing for the great deceiver that steals men's brains
and opens the door to every kind of tragedy.

Does he, as a minister, have certain professional standards
of conduct which he must ever keep in mind? Yes, and they
ought to be more definitely understood. Here are the ten
commandments of ministerial ethics as I see them:

(1) *No sheep-stealing!* The minister must never deflect
people from loyalty to their church in order to build
up his own.

(2) *No tale-bearing!* If he knows or hears anything to
the discredit of another minister he should either keep
silent about it or go directly to the minister concerned
or, if necessary, to his responsible ecclesiastical su-
periors, and to no one else.

(3) *Loyalty to his predecessor!* He will never be in any
way a candidate for a church until the incumbent minister has resigned. He will not take too seriously criticisms he hears about his predecessor, remembering that
similar tales follow every pastorate. They reveal the
disgruntled or the ingratiating.

(4) *Consideration for his successor!* He will try to leave
ample and accurate records, an organization set up and
going, and a spirit of anticipatory good will for the
man who is to follow him. Then he will keep out of
parish affairs and return for no funerals or weddings

except in cooperation with or because of the absence of his successor. Give the man who succeeds you a real chance to succeed!

(5) *Play the game with the ecclesiastical authorities!* The minister is part of a denomination and, beyond that, of the church universal. As a representative of organized Christianity he cannot be a " lone wolf." He owes his education and security in part to a Christian fellowship which he in turn should support and strengthen.

(6) *Be a good citizen!* As a minister he is ordinarily exempt from jury duty and military service. All the more, therefore, must he contribute his share in all appropriate good works for the common good. But his chief public service will be rendered as a fair, free and fearless voice speaking truth in love on all matters of public welfare where he is qualified to speak at all.

(7) *Devote full time to the job!* He has to punch no time clock and his product cannot be weighed and measured. But he must be sure he earns his salary and sets an example of honest work and loyal service.

(8) *Serve regardless of compensation!* No true minister will charge for his services. If he cannot live on the support given let him say so to some trusted leader, but he will make no demands. He will serve all regardless of compensation. He may be impecunious but never mercenary. In addition to salary he may receive payment for articles and outside addresses, also royalties for books he has written, providing these things do not encroach upon his regular duties. Wedding fees he turns over to his wife — and requires from her

no accounting. Funeral fees he does not accept from his parishioners. From outsiders they may be accepted — practice differs — but, many ministers stipulate, only as contributions to some charitable fund.

(9) *Remember the minister's special responsibility regarding women!* His work in general, and his pastoral calling in particular, give him a privileged position. It must never be abused. Slander and gossip may end his usefulness if they have any basis either in reality or only in careless indiscretion. He must never quarrel with a woman, on the one hand, and should avoid all familiarities, on the other. He had better not call even his secretary by her first name. If there is no foolishness in his dealings with women he will gain in greater measure the love and respect of all — men as well as women. There is nothing which depresses a church so much as any hint of scandal about the minister.

(10) *Make a success of home!* Sometimes the minister's home is his greatest success. Sons of ministers outnumber proportionally the sons of any other profession in achieving a place in *Who's Who,* in happy refutation of popular misconceptions about them. The leading layman in many a church is a son of an earlier pastor. But the minister must remember that his wife and children live in the glare of pitiless publicity. They suffer acutely at times from a reaction due to his vocation. Therefore he owes it to his home to be especially loyal, considerate and tender. If his home is a manifest success the welfare of all homes in his parish increases. If his home fails — but I forbear!

If you have survived this chapter and the
ministry still glows for you as a great vocation, you are ready at last to consider
how to prepare for the task.

CHAPTER SEVEN

THE MINISTER'S TRAINING

IDEALLY, a man's training for any profession ought to begin about a hundred years before he is born, but that is difficult to arrange. Sometimes men with three generations of the culture and discipline of the Christian parsonage behind them turn out to be aviators or politicians, and all that training is lost — so far as the ministry is concerned. Then, on the other hand, up out of mine or factory or farm comes a youth with little churchly background but with an authentic vision that will not be denied. We have to make ministers out of the men who recognize a call when it comes to them.

What is a call to the ministry and what makes it possible? A call to the ministry is not ordinarily, or preferably, a spectacular emotional experience, although sometimes pent up emotions and delayed decisions may finally register themselves in one dramatic moment never to be forgotten. With far more ministers, however, the call has been an adventurous hope and a growing conviction that here at last is a vocation into which one could put all he had and find great joy and reward in doing so. Professor George Herbert Palmer used to say, concerning his love of teaching, that Harvard University paid him for doing something for the privilege of doing which he would gladly have paid Harvard University, had that been necessary. When a man, after having had enough experience to judge, feels that way about any profession there is little doubt that he has been " called." God gives us joy and suffering in the tasks we were meant to do, and the two are close akin.

It would be better, however, not to judge the validity of one's call to the ministry by purely emotional reactions, though the emotions are wiser than some people think. A certain amount of self-analysis is possible. Let the young man ask himself, not " Do I look well in a pulpit? " or " Am I conspicuously pious and unusually fluent in religious talk? " or " Do all the old ladies think I'd be a lovely minister? " — but rather more searching questions like these: " Am I willing to tackle four years of college and three years of graduate study? " " Can I do good enough intellectual work to justify what all that education will cost me or someone else? " " Do I really love folks enough and am I sufficiently concerned for human welfare to abandon all dreams of wealth or power and devote myself to service? " " How competent am I or can I become in English, history, sociology, psychology and public speaking? " and finally, " Have I any real and kindling enthusiasm for Jesus and his philosophy of life? "

But self-analysis suffers notoriously from blind spots; so check up your " call " with some competent and trusted adviser. He may be a pastor, a high school teacher, a college professor, an editor or a businessman — preferably one who has been to college. He will want to know what alternatives you have considered and why you rejected them, and what about the minister's job you really know. He will ask you if you have read this book! Let us hope he is direct and courageous enough to give you his honest reaction. But, even so, his direction is not final, one way or the other.

There is still a third way of checking up and that is by a trial trip. Many a man has not made his final vocational decision until a year in the seminary and a summer on his own

in charge of a little home missionary church out on the plains
or up in the mountains have given him the " feel " of the
thing and shown him its realities.

One thing is certain: the decision for or against the ministry ought never to be made on financial grounds. Don't give
up the ministry because of poverty. There is always some
way of earning your way through college and seminary if
you mean business. And, on the other hand, the man who
chooses the ministry because it seems to be a comparatively
easy financial road to an education will only clutter up some
theological seminary and lose his own self-respect in the end,
unless he happens to get converted somewhere along the way.

Studies in theological education reveal that the most
promising students are often those who did not wake up to
the possibilities of the ministry until late in their college
career. There is something to be said for late-blooming varieties. Such students thought that they were headed for
engineering or law or architecture, until a course in English
poetry or sociology or philosophy, or a glimpse at the back
alleys of a city slum, or a talk in chapel finally woke them up.
Then they saw some gleam of the glorious possibilities of the
Christian church which has served humanity through the centuries and is still calling for young men to carry on that service today. They discovered they were most concerned about
human engineering and the laws of God and the architecture
of things to come.

But it would be dangerous to depend solely on the late-
blooming varieties for our supply of ministers. Many a man
who wakes up to the ministry as a possible vocation about his
senior year in college, or even after three years in a law school
or a graduate school of business administration, could have
been saved a good deal of time if the nature of the ministry

had been adequately presented to him in high school. After all, that is when youth more frequently makes up its mind on basic questions than the world realizes. Now while colleges may have departments of religion and considerable organized Christian work, the high school is almost entirely secular, and such vocational guidance as the high school gives is likely to ignore the ministry entirely. This is a critical weakness in the church's strategy for securing strong leadership. Something ought to be done about it, the program varying according to the local situations and the cooperation possible between the local pastors and the high school principal.

What kind of college should the prospective minister choose? There is no definite answer. For a certain type of student the small college, if it fosters high scholarship, is admirable and produces good results. And yet it must be said that a certain maturity and tough-mindedness seem to be developed best in a university atmosphere. If the pretheological student can survive at the university he has proved his hardiness and probably need not be worried about it any further.

What shall the pretheological student study in college? Some would say, Everything except religion! To follow that exaggerated advice would be very dangerous. True, the student had better not major in religion, but a good basic Bible course is as important for him at that stage as for anyone else. College is his golden opportunity, however, to get a grasp on literature, history, sociology, philosophy and psychology. He had better emphasize these broadly cultural subjects, majoring in one of them and not forgetting to include at least one good laboratory course in science, preferably biology. The minister needs to know and appreciate the scientific attack

upon a problem. As to languages, he may take enough to
profit by their discipline in ordered thinking and discover
whether he wants to go further along the linguistic road.

Then, too, there is no reason why the student should lose
himself completely in books and studies. Not all of a college
education is acquired in the classroom. At our seminary we
are proud of the cheerleaders, athletes, editors, star actors,
debaters and headwaiters who have decided to go into the
ministry. But we are still waiting for our first drum major
or cadet colonel!

Certain widely prevalent misconceptions about the theological seminary itself need to be cleared away. Many a student, brought up in the academic freedom and clear white
light of truth as it shines on the college campus, hesitates to
plunge into the murky pool of theological dogmatism. He
has a hazy traditional idea that a seminary is a cloistered back-
water of life, a dismal place where sour-visaged theologians
ram outworn doctrines down the student's throat and de-
nounce him as a poor lost soul if he raises any questions or
objections. Or else he fears that the seminary will be so out
of touch with life that he might as well be living in Tibet.

Nothing could be more unrealistic. As a matter of fact,
the modern theological seminary, frequently located adjacent
to or connected with a great university, is as searchingly
scientific in spirit and methods as any other professional
school or graduate department. All problems are ap-
proached historically, all the pros and cons are fearlessly presented, no dogmatic hedges prevent the freest analysis and
debate. The student comes out where he chooses to come
out after all the evidence is in. He is graded according to his
knowledge of the facts and his ability to handle them, not by

his conformity to a narrow orthodoxy. His particular denomination may hold him up on points of doctrine later on, but the seminary is mainly concerned with stimulating him to " prove all things," which means, to test all things, " and hold fast to that which is good."

In general, the modern school of the prophets has four great disciplines by which it seeks to train the minister of tomorrow. The first of these comprises the whole background of religion — what it is, what its historical development has been, what it has to say about the great problems of life. This discipline will always make up the bulk of the student's academic work. It includes study of the Bible, church history, Christian theology, the history and philosophy of religion.

Only with such a sound historical training can the minister wisely and sanely evaluate and withstand some of the surface vagaries of the modern mind as well as appreciate and cooperate with its deeper-running currents of constructive purpose. Contemporary charlatans, demagogues and fanatics can sometimes best be understood and analyzed by comparison with their prototypes of other days whose complete record is now on file in the archives of history. A doctrine or an idea which the student has traced through its whole historical development is less likely to result in fanaticism or intolerance, while its real values, if any, will survive because freed from temporary wrappings and local coloring. Background — historical, theological, biblical, philosophical background — is what a scholarly seminary training ought to give a minister, not just a few snappy sermon outlines, a cocksure dogmatism, and a bag of tricks which could be learned under clever teachers in about six weeks.

The second discipline is sociological. The minister must face the major ethical problems of modern life and learn to analyze its social trends. He must understand the social facts and forces that surge around the rock of ages on which his church is founded. He must, therefore, study social ethics, trends in rural and urban life as they affect the church, problems of family and vocational life, and the sociology of religion. He cannot preach the social gospel all the time. No, but he can't omit it all the time either. So he had better be trained to preach it intelligently and keep his facts ahead of his oratory.

The third discipline, both newest and oldest of all, is the psychological. It is a perfectly sound belief, isn't it, that a minister ought to know something about the soul? Well, the modern name for " soul " is " human personality," and psychology is one key to its understanding. Hence the courses in mental hygiene and character development, in personality disorders and pastoral counseling. For these courses our particular seminary, for example, calls in a chaplain from a mental hospital, and also gives selected students an opportunity to study in the hospital under his direction.

The fourth great area of theological preparation includes all those practical disciplines by which the student learns to do the actual work of a minister. These include courses in preaching, church administration, worship, religious drama, literature and biography, music, religious education and public speaking. But, since the most effective learning is by doing, these subjects are supplemented by carefully supervised field work. All during his course the student has responsibility for certain definite tasks in church, Sunday school, social settlement, research projects or rural areas. He is visited " on location " by the director of field work, who is a full-time faculty member trained for that service, and later he reports and discusses the living problems encountered in the day's work at a field work seminar meeting one evening every week. When summer comes the student's field work may take him to far distant states, but he returns with new insights into his vocation and deeper interest in his classroom opportunities.

Usually at about the end of his first year in seminary the student applies to his denomination for a license to preach. The granting of a license involves an examination by the proper ecclesiastical authorities and is the first step toward the ordination, which is preceded by a more thorough and searching examination. The ordination, of course, is his goal after his seminary course is over and he has secured his professional degree of bachelor of divinity, B.D. It seems anomalous that after three years of graduate work the student should receive only another bachelor's degree while the young lawyer may claim his J.D., doctor of jurisprudence; and so some seminaries would like to change the B.D. degree to a Th.D., doctor of theology. Certainly the student has worked as hard and learned as much as his college classmate who after three years may be receiving his Ph.D., doctor of philosophy, with a thesis on " The Use of the Comma in the Punctuation of Medieval Icelandic Literature " or some similarly remote subject of alleged research. But the important thing is to be a " doctor," that is, a learned man, whether the diploma is inscribed with that title or not.

Travel should not be neglected as an important element in the training of a minister. Many seminaries award to the most capable student of each year's graduating class a greatly prized fellowship which provides for one or two years' study and travel abroad. Such study used to be undertaken largely in German universities, but under the present regimentation of scholarship in that country students in search of academic freedom will probably turn to the British universities, such as Oxford, Cambridge, London and Edinburgh, which also have the advantage of no very difficult language barriers. There are barriers, but they are not insurmountable! The long vacations customary abroad also give the student a great cultural opportunity for travel on the Continent and especially to the Holy Land. Even if the student does not win such a prize for foreign study he ought by all means as soon as possible to see Egypt, Italy, Greece and Palestine. All antiquity, and especially his studies in the Bible, will glow for him with new reality after such a journey.

But foreign travel is not the only kind which may broaden the parson's outlook and add depth and color to his preaching. In these days of open roads and inexpensive cars, tourist camps and trailers, he ought to see his own country. Historic spots and scenic beauty are important but so also is a first-hand sight and understanding of the squalor of city slums and bleak mining camps and the desolation of sharecroppers' cabins. These will leave him only enraged or disheartened unless he also sees the gleams of a nobler civilization in those lighthouses of human brotherhood which he should also search out and visit — such as the Chicago Commons and Hull House, the Delta Farms in Mississippi, Berea College in Kentucky, Tillotson College for Negroes in Texas and many another venture in cooperative living and invincible good will. In that seminary which I know best of all the students go on a " spring hike " during Easter vacation, trekking across the country in a string of nondescript automobiles and visiting everything from the TVA to a farmers' strike in Iowa. It is one way to test one's education!

Finally, it should hardly need to be said that the minister's education and training are never ended. He must read new books and think new thoughts and face new issues all his life long. If he does he will remain perennially young — witness Graham Taylor writing his weekly column for the *Chicago Daily News* at the age of eighty-six and still bubbling over with vitality and contemporary understanding. The summer schools and pastors' institutes or ministers' weeks now provided by so many seminaries and other agencies also conspire to keep the pastor who attends them mentally alert, resilient and up to date.

Isn't this minister's job a great task? But it's too big for any one person, you say? True enough, and that is one reason why almost all ministers are married. Hence the next chapter!

CHAPTER EIGHT

THE MINISTER'S WIFE

SOME MINISTERS succeed gloriously in their professional careers without a wife, and occasionally a minister fails because of a wife who simply could not adjust herself to the job. Phillips Brooks never married and of course the pope is a bachelor. Nevertheless, after an experience of over thirty years, with a good deal of observation on the side, I heartily recommend that the minister be married. Most churches take it for granted that he will be. The parsonage is one of the unique institutions of Protestantism; those who speak as though all the psychological advantages were on the side of the Roman Catholic priest with his confessional, his sacerdotal status and his authoritative relationship to his congregation perhaps forget that Protestantism also has its appropriate and unique institutions and traditions, not least of them the minister's home in the heart of the parish.

Where shall the minister find his wife? Perhaps the wisest answer would be, where she finds him. After all, courtship is a mutual affair. Some of the happiest solutions to this part of life's problem, however, are made in college or even in the theological seminary — where these institutions are, happily, coeducational. I am not saying that the minister's wife must be a college graduate. That would be a very external and superficial criterion. Some of the wisest, most gracious and truly cultured women who ever lived never went to college. A college diploma is no guarantee of the graces and wisdom needed in the parsonage. And yet, on the whole, other things being equal, the pastor's wife who is a college graduate has a better start than the one who is not. The rest depends upon her insight, character and social genius. College can develop these qualities but not create them. They are native endowments or at least social inheritances. In general it is safe to say that the young woman whose native ability and good sense are reinforced by a knowledge that she has had as good educational advantages as the other women of the church, together with the incidental social and organizational experience which college gives, will begin her career in the parsonage with more confidence and understanding than one who lacks this background.

Some girls shrink from the thought of ever being a minister's wife and not a few parents zealously guard their daughters from any contact with theological students lest this strange and untoward fate befall them. Because such fears rest largely upon false assumptions and inadequate knowledge of life in a parsonage, let us look for a while at the job of the minister's wife. In the opinion of the two people whose joint experience lies back of this chapter it is one of the happiest, most worth-while lives a woman can lead.

First of all, the minister's wife should be what every other married woman would wish to be, a homemaker. As the mistress of the manse she is the center of the most significant home in the parish. If she is not interested in creating a home where peace, joy and order reign, a refuge from the strident vulgar outside world and a training ground for character, a home with children in it, a home given to hospitality and built on mutual confidence and utter loyalty, then she had better not marry at all. And particularly she had better not

marry a minister. For if the home she makes has these qualities, its unconscious, unpremeditated influence will quietly
radiate throughout the parish and reinforce all the joint ministry of her husband and herself. But if it has them not the
minister will suffer such a handicap as will almost certainly
ruin his career or, through the battle to rise above it, make
him a very great soul indeed. But in either case his wife will
be utterly miserable.

An ideal home is not one in which there are no disagree-
ments, no tensions of opinion or desire, no suffering or sorrow, but one in which there is absolute basic loyalty and complete confidence and trust. Love is so vague and sentimental
a word that it needs to be translated into these more prosaic
terms. If there is any cloud of misunderstanding or distrust
between the parson and his wife, you may depend upon it
that the parish will not be long in sensing it. It will be well,
therefore, if minister and wife both live lives which are an
open book wherein anyone may read. " Fierce is the light
that beats upon a throne " — and a parsonage. But this
frankness in itself is a considerable protection and guarantee
of happiness to married life. It means that husband and wife
have no secrets from each other, no flirtations or entangle-
ments, no half-loyalties.

Once in a certain city a prominent minister was under fire.
His fearless advocacy of civic decency had won him the
hatred of powerful sinister forces in the community. An at-
tempt to besmirch his name by alleged scandal threatened.
His church board met with him to consider the situation.
The whole community was stirred with apprehension.
Everything cleared up when he quietly said: " I have done
nothing dishonorable. My wife is here. She knows all the

circumstances. We have no secrets from each other. There
is no disharmony between us. She is absolutely and unre-
servedly with me in facing this situation." Nothing more
needed to be said. The church backed up their minister, the
attacking forces retreated, the alleged scandal was never pub-
lished. But suppose that minister had not been protected by
a good wife and a happy married relationship; what a tragedy
he might have faced!

As the presiding genius in the home, the minister's wife is
to a degree inevitably his social secretary. She may indeed
often supply the background of social *savoir faire* which her
husband, good man and true though he may be, possibly
never acquired in his home or college or even in the theological seminary. After all, what mere man really knows how
to give a tea or in whose honor, or how to have the deacons in
to dinner, or give a party for the young people? If a young
woman likes to do these things the position of minister's wife
opens up almost unlimited possibilities to her. On the other
hand, she may not be much of a social butterfly and prefer to
organize study groups or work in the child-guidance clinic
or coach the drama club. But whichever way her talents lead,
her social opportunities are probably greater than those of
any other woman in the community.

Nor does social life necessarily involve large expense if one
has the wit and originality to do things simply. In a California city years ago one of the most delightful social occasions of the season was a series of Sunday noon luncheons
which a resourceful host and hostess used to give under the
fig tree in their back yard with bacon, scrambled eggs and
coffee for the menu, all cooked and served outdoors.

In order that this chapter may not be just a man's reaction

to the topic under consideration I have asked the minister's
wife I know best of all to set down some of her ideas on the
subject — and here they are.

" The life of a minister's wife is most interesting first of all
because it is so intimately bound up with her husband's.
Few married couples can share so much. Again, it often involves a good deal of travel and variety in places of residence.
We all like to ' go places ' and see the country, and the minister's career does not ordinarily keep him in just one spot for
life. As a friend of mine remarked, ' Here I've got to stick
in little old New York while you are moving from Maine to
California and even the islands of the sea.'

" Of course, in traveling from place to place in the course
of a lifetime, one gathers and enjoys a great group of friends.
Moreover, church people represent a cross section of society
and as one has friends in all groups one comes to know and
understand a wide variety of people. On the whole it is a
privilege to be linked up with a great group of church women
who are, as someone has called them, ' the aristocracy of the
race ' — an aristocracy of character, service and devotion.
Church people have the international mind; they have com-
parative freedom from race prejudice; their interests and sympathies reach out far beyond their own doorstep. Thus the
minister's wife is fortunate in the people she can work with.

" There are certain limitations, of course, which the minister's wife may as well make up her mind to accept. She can
possess few *things* — moving about settles that. And she
must have an adaptable mind, putting up philosophically in
one parish with a parsonage that has ten great lofty rooms
and in the next with one that has only six, and making no

demands nor letting her soul be ruffled by these things. Financially she will have just enough to live on to place her as well as the average woman in her church. Hence she needs to be ingenious about the management of her home. But in that she has lots of company.

" Many things are expected of her. At a recent gathering the question was asked: What do you consider your most important job as minister's wife? Answers such as these came in: ' To be a hostess in my home to the church folk '; ' To take care of my family '; ' To be a buffer between my husband and the public '; ' To secure Sunday school teachers '; ' To keep my mouth shut when I'd like to say something '; ' To support my husband in the program of the church.'

" As a potential leader in the women's work in the church the minister's wife should keep herself informed on what up-to-date churches are doing in this field of activity. She should know what program material is available and what type of organization is most effective. She can do this ordinarily by active cooperation with the denominational organization of women in her area and with other women's organizations devoted to special interests such as peace or civic welfare or missions. In this way she will become well informed so that her judgment will be of value when she is consulted as to programs, projects and organization.

" She needs to be alert to new methods and have wisdom in suggesting changes. She will discover that, on the whole, church women alter their organizational set-up with great travail of spirit; most of them are fearful of changes. In a world of changes this seems most pathetic. Hence the value of a committee on survey and reorganization to be commissioned in every church at least once in every five years. Meanwhile the minister's wife should visit other denominational groups, as opportunity offers, on the lookout for new ideas and methods. A recent survey of churches east and west brought to light a church group named the 'Ladies' Benevolent Association.' It would doubtless give some of the ladies concerned great anguish to change that name but they might well ask themselves what hope there would be of a modern up-to-date college girl's caring to be a member of such an association. Probably this name is itself an improvement upon the original 'Female Benevolent Association,' but it now ought to be improved still further.

" Should the minister's wife hold office in the women's group in her church; especially, should she be the president? There is much against it, for if she does so it means that one person less from the group itself is being interested and trained to carry responsibility. She ought rather to stand behind the president, helping her in every way. However, she should master one thing in particular, namely, parliamentary law, so that under her guidance meetings of church women will be conducted with an order and dignity fully equal to those of any club. She can also help quietly behind the scenes by being ever on the lookout for good leadership material among the women of the church, suggesting names to the nominating committee and getting the right type of women fitted to the various offices and tasks.

" The Sunday school also will claim her help. Perhaps she will grow up with the school as her own children progress through it, though normally she will probably be especially well equipped to work with the high school age group, one of the most important and at the same time most difficult of all ages in the school. As she grows older, it is to be hoped she will be awake when the time arrives for her to give herself more to the adults and secure younger leadership for

youth. Besides her church activities, she ought to have time
to work in some worth-while organizations like the League
of Women Voters, the College Club or the local Woman's
Club.

" If all that has been outlined seems too big a task, nevertheless it can be done. Helpful, noble ways of living day by
day seem to open up before one who will put the really great
and noble things in life first and not be lost in a maze of
trivial and superficial interests.

" Quite recently a certain minister changed his parish.
One member of the congregation which he was leaving was
heard to remark, ' I'm not concerned about the next minister
we get, but I know we'll never find another Mrs. Blank ' —
the minister's wife. Of course, there are just as many good
ministers' wives as there are good ministers, but it was a well
deserved tribute. Many a minister has had a happier pastorate than he knows because the people loved his wife."

Continuing now on my own account, may I suggest some
very definite ways in which a wife can help her husband in
this intricate task of the Christian ministry? There is for
instance the matter of pastoral counseling. People come to
you for advice on all sorts of matters. Usually what they
bring up first is not the real subject of their quest. They first
just try to discover your general attitude. But finally they
may bring up a problem that at first seems too big for you.
Don't let it. Play for time and contrive to consult your wife
before answering. The insights of a good woman are not
infallible, but no discriminating man will disregard them.
The habit of talking things over with his wife fully and un-
reservedly is one very important for a parson to cultivate.

She will not betray him if she is an intelligent woman, whereas her hunches and intuitions will often save him from foolishness and failure.

Should the minister's wife help him with his sermons? Some wives do a great deal in this respect. They read books, collect illustrations, suggest topics and, horrible to relate, even have the sermon preached to them in advance. I have never considered this last procedure quite sportsmanlike. The minister's wife ought to have the privilege of hearing the sermon fresh and unspoiled, just as members of the congregation do. In general I think the less responsibility she has for the preaching the better. She has enough responsibility in other matters and the minister had better shoulder this burden alone, except for such help as she volunteers. Of course she will be invaluable as a critic — but there let her, in turn, beware! To preach every Sunday is a hard enough task, and there are times when the soul of a creative artist who already senses his shortcomings can stand criticism, and there are times when it cannot. I would suggest to all ministers' wives this rule: Never omit any criticism because you fear wounding your husband. Both of you should remember that " faithful are the wounds of a friend." But, at the same time, it will be better to make note of your intended criticism and reserve it until about Tuesday morning.

What perils attend the career of the minister's wife? Three major ones: professionalism, lack of tact, and overwork. All must be guarded against. By professionalism I mean always talking about the church as well as assuming a sanctimonious attitude in voice and conduct and, I almost said, in dress. The minister's wife should remember that she is first of all a human being, and that pretty clothes are essential for a normal woman. Fortunately the day has gone by when she was expected to select nothing but black or grey and wear a bonnet.

As to tact, there is no formula for it. Diplomacy has been defined as the gentle art of letting other people have your way. But tact is either inherent or else is learned more or less imperfectly in the school of hard knocks. Only let them be knocks received but never given! Here the text, " It is more blessed to give than to receive," does not apply.

But when it comes to overwork, the matter is largely one of good judgment, organization and will power. No over-worked person can do his best and a crisis may find him tired, peevish, slow of apprehension. Hence the necessity so to organize your life as to have regular hours of sleep, definite rest periods, adequate recreation and genuinely relaxing vacations. If you haven't enough intelligence to manage these things, you ought to punch a time clock and not attempt anything so exacting as the creative tasks which the minister and his wife confront together. These are glittering generalities and each person must translate them into terms of practical daily living.

But, on the other hand, don't be lazy or self-indulgent. It is a great and holy spiritual battle in which you are engaged. This critical day of the world's history is no time in which to give to the cause of Christ less than one's best even to the uttermost ounce of effort.

Can the minister and his wife have a social life apart from the church? It is almost necessary that they should. Toward the church members they must of course be absolutely impartial. Great social intimacy with one family or group is likely to be resented by others. Happy the community in which the various ministers and their wives can form a congenial group, bound together by common professional interests. The best intimate friends for the minister and his wife are another minister and his wife. Such friendships suggest no favoritism inside the parish and arouse no antagonism.

Moreover, the minister and his wife for this same reason are especially dependent on each other and on their children for their intimate social life. They need to take one day a week, if possible — say Saturday afternoon and Monday morning — to get out of the parish and have a change of scene. Just a trip to the theater will do. And, if they can own a secluded cabin in the hills or beside a river, or an abandoned farm, that is better still. For years, in Hawaii, I went swimming with my children Saturday afternoons and played tennis with three fellow ministers on Monday mornings. How to take the family off the job on a holiday is one of the fine arts of being a minister's wife.

But, before the chapter ends, someone is sure to ask, But did the church hire the minister's wife? The answer is, No! And while her children are little the minister's wife will not be able to do more church work than any other young mother. Nevertheless, it is only good sportsmanship on her part to give to the service of the church as much time and energy as other women members similarly situated are giving.

Some women say: My job is to make a good home for my husband and my responsibility ends there; the doctor's wife isn't expected to run the hospital. But the woman who takes that attitude will lose a great deal of fun, for being a minister's wife is in itself a career. It is really a sort of unique profession and the woman who realizes its possibilities will find it a very rewarding life indeed. Many young women today, when they find that they are going to marry ministers, go to seminary or training school and take courses in Bible, religious education, mental hygiene, pageantry and religious drama, so as to be prepared to make the most of the opportunities church work will open to them. They become community-minded; life's larger horizons beckon to them, and they discover that the minister's wife may become one of the key women of the community in which she lives.

Mrs. Roosevelt has demonstrated what a career it may be to be the wife of a president of the United States. Why not regard the position of minister's wife as an opportunity for a career?

But perhaps before searching for a wife the prospective minister had better sit down and subject himself to careful self-examination. The next chapter will tell him how to go about it.

CHAPTER NINE

A SELF-ANALYSIS FOR MINISTERS

HAVING surveyed the minister's job, perhaps the minister, or prospective minister, might find it interesting, in closing, to survey himself. Many a man will ask himself: How well suited am I to a pastor's life and responsibilities? How can I estimate my powers and measure my capacities and temperament?

The following outline of personal self-measurement may help. It has been prepared by a committee of the American Association of Theological Schools to assist faculties and students in estimating personality development at about the end of the first year in the theological seminary. But it is capable of much more extended use. Many a senior in college might well check himself against it, and not a few men well along in the work of the ministry will find it highly entertaining to do so.

Remember that the work of the Christian church is not carried by paragons of perfection, that people have both the virtues and defects of their qualities, and that drive and purpose in the end often count for more than mere talent or endowment.

This is not an " objective " test. It cannot be " scored." However, you can grade yourself by underscoring the descriptive term which comes nearest to accuracy in your case. In many instances you will mark more than one descriptive term since the terms used are not always mutually exclusive.

And, if you distrust your own appraisal of yourself, have some wise counselor, some intelligent devoted friend, check your estimate and so help you to a more secure judgment.

I. PHYSIQUE AND PERSONAL APPEARANCE

(1) *Unusual physical traits.*

> Note any unusual physical traits such as height, weight, deformity, etc., which may distract attention, impede normal activity, or otherwise interfere with effectiveness.

(2) *Physical vitality.*

> Too low. Limited endurance. Fairly vigorous. Superior endurance. Rugged.

(3) *Output of energy.*

> Lazy. Never exerts himself seriously.
> Normal output of energy.
> Overenergetic with appearance of rushing.
> Constantly at work with good economy of energy.

(4) *Voice.*

> Gruff. Dull and flat. Staccato.
> Loud. Natural. Pleasing.

(5) *Speech.*

> Stutters. Lisps. Stammers.
> Natural. Clear and easily heard.

(6) *Dress.*

> Ungroomed. Untidy. Overdressed. Neat.

(7) *Cleanliness.*

> Unpleasant impression. Neutral impression.
> Pleasing impression.

(8) *Appearance of room.*

> Untidy. Average. Unusually well kept.

(9) *Manliness.*

> Very effeminate in appearance and bearing.
> Effeminate in appearance and bearing.
> Masculine in appearance and bearing.
> Unusually masculine in appearance and bearing.

(10) *Personal habits.*
> Note any personal habits which may interfere with career.

II. MENTAL AND TEMPERAMENTAL

(11) *Intelligence.*
> Intelligence test score if known.
> Or estimate: Backward (IQ 80–89. Normal (90–109).
> Bright (110–119). Very bright (120–129). Very superior (130–).

(12) *Type of personality.*
> Definitely introvertive. Tendency toward introversion.
> Tendency toward extraversion. Definitely extravertive.
> Well balanced.

(13) *Temperament* (underscore one of the five, and the adjective which comes nearest describing the characteristic mood).
> Sanguine: ardent, confident, hopeful.
> Choleric: easily fretted, irritable, easily angered, irascible.
> Melancholic: easily depressed, melancholy.
> Phlegmatic: sluggish, apathetic, cool, composed.
> Nervous: tense, keyed up, excitable, highly excitable.

(14) *Judgment.*
> No sense of values or relations. Conclusions frequently wrong.
> Average common sense. Judges quickly and well.
> Judgment unusually sound.

(15) *Intellectual honesty.*
> Will never give up a position once taken.
> Labeling a man or an idea (" modernist," " fundamentalist," etc.) settles an argument for him.
> Readily recognizes truth in a position from which he differs.
> Devoted to truth wherever found.
> Fearless advocate of truth as he sees it, at whatever cost.

(16) *Ability to learn.*
> Learns very slowly. Learns slowly. Average.
> Learns rapidly. Learns very rapidly.

(Specify different abilities in various kinds of learning if this is important.)

(17) *Industriousness in academic work.*

Lazy. Just gets by. Average worker.

Good worker. Very hard worker.

(Specify differing industry in various fields if important.)

(18) *Interest in academic work.*

Uninterested. Slight interest. Average.

Good interest. Absorbed.

(Specify differing interests in various fields if important.)

(19) *Attitudes toward academic work.*

A chore to be done grudgingly. Does only what is required.

Pleasing general attitude. Eager for new knowledge.

Noted for superior work.

(Specify differing attitudes in various fields if important.)

(20) *Attitudes toward faculty teaching.*

Accepts unthinkingly. Seeks support for ideas already held.

Sharply critical. Likes to take opposite view.

Will entertain new ideas but only slowly.

Weighs discriminatingly and accepts when convinced.

(Specify differing attitudes toward various professors if important.)

(21) *Habits of thinking.*

Will not face problems. Follows others' thinking.

Thinks when forced to. Independent thinker.

Independent and creative thinker.

(22) *Attitude toward responsibility.*

Accepts grudgingly. Forgets it.

Average. Accepts heartily.

Always discharges it.

(23) *Independence.*

Has to have everything done for him.

Overdependent on some person (specify).

So independent he cannot receive help gracefully.

Excessive desire to appear different.

Fully able to take care of himself.

(24) *Freshness of thought.*
> Dry as dust in his expression of thought.
> Distracts attention by his rhetoric.
> Says the trite thing.
> Clear and fresh expression of thought.
> Striking originality.

III. SOCIAL QUALITIES

(25) *Ability to meet people of varying types.*
> Very poor. Poor. Average.
> Above average. Very unusual.

(26) *Disposition toward social contacts.*
> Recluse. Unable to be alone. Mingles naturally.
> Known for ability to make wholesome social contacts.

(27) *Adaptability in varying social situations.*
> Very poor. Poor. Average.
> Above average. Very unusual.

(28) *Ability to work with persons of diverse views.*
> Quickly in conflict.
> Conceals own views for sake of harmony.
> Not satisfied unless others hold his views.
> Outspoken but considerate of others' views.
> Can lead people of divergent views to common action.

(29) *Attitude in personal association.*
> Very reserved. Stiffly dignified.
> Easily offended. Absent-minded.
> Wins confidence readily. Draws out the best in people.

(30) *Presence.*
> Nervous. Fidgets with something. Shy. Forward.
> Averted eyes. Self-possessed.

(31) *Courtesy in conversation.*
> Rude. Tries to do all the talking. Difficult to draw out.
> Good listener. Pleasant to talk with.
> Leaves impression of being unusually good conversationalist.

(32) *Observance of social conventions.*
> Frequently does "the wrong thing."

Does not profit by opportunity to learn social usage.
Seems unconcerned. Reasonably tactful.
Always does " the right thing."

(33) *Sense of humor.*

None whatever. Practical joker. Overdeveloped sense of humor.
Wholesome sense of humor. Tells a good story at the apt time.

(34) *Attitude toward persons of other sex.*

Has occasioned unfavorable comment. Loves a smutty story.
Too free. Diffident. Stiff and too conventional.
Natural and wholesome. Has occasioned favorable comment.

(35) *Punctuality in appointments.*

Forgets appointments. Frequently late.
Ahead of time. Punctual.

(36) *Punctuality in academic responsibilities.*

Frequently behind time with assignments.
Good at making excuses.
Usually on time with work.
Always on time with work.

(37) *Attitude toward public opinion.*

Controlled by it. Likes to scandalize it.
Defies it. Indifferent. Normally influenced by it.
Seeks to shape it for his own ends.
Seeks to shape it for unselfish ends.

(38) *Reputation.*

Under suspicion. Weak under temptation. Keeps word when given.
Very dependable. Notably conscientious.

(39) *Insight into social conditions* (as war, race conflict, etc.).

No interest. Evades the real issues.
Merely academic interest.
Known for partisan interest.
Active interest commanding general respect.
(Specify particulars if important.)

(40) *Sincerity.*

> Makes frequent impression of insincerity.
> Sincerity occasionally open to question.
> Wholly sincere.

(41) *Considerateness.*

> Seems never to consider circumstances of others.
> Considers others when wants something from them.
> Fairly considerate.
> Frequently doing thoughtful acts.
> Seems always to sense circumstances of others and act accordingly.

(42) *Cooperation.*

> Not cooperative.
> " Cannot cooperate because must be loyal to convictions."
> Cooperates moderately. Happy in cooperative work.
> Cooperates excellently without sacrifice of conviction.

(43) *Capacity for friendship.*

> Has no close friends. Has very few close friends.
> Has many real friends. Has a genius for friendship.

(44) *Leadership.*

> Antagonizes people. Gains little support.
> Plans successfully for others.
> Organizes and directs others acceptably.
> Commands confidence and leads group notably.

IV. RELIGIOUS LIFE

(45) *Attitude toward self.*

> Very selfish. Cocky. False humility (Uriah Heep).
> Usually forgets self. True simple humility (St. Francis).

(46) *Genuineness of religious life.*

> Depends on others for religious experience.
> Depends on religious forms which mean little to him.
> Overtalkative about his own religious experience.
> Groping for experience of God.
> Gives unintentional impression he knows God in his own experience.

(47) *Discernment of spiritual values.*
>Chiefly concerned with one doctrine.
>A legalistic view of religion.
>Chiefly interested in the letter of religion.
>Chiefly concerned with central realities of gospel.
>Utterly devoted to central realities of gospel.

(48) *Range of religious thought.*
>Has one theological hobby.
>Meager range of religious ideas.
>Range of religious ideas just like those of people with whom he associates.
>Wide range of interest in all matters relating to religion.
>Intelligent discernment in all matters relating to religion.

(49) *Attitude toward new and old in religious thought.*
>Contemptuous of " new " religious ideas.
>Contemptuous of " old " religious ideas.
>Especially interested in " new " religious ideas.
>Especially interested in " old " religious ideas.
>Interested in truth no matter when first discerned.

(50) *Attitude toward religious leaders.*
>Overcritical. Awed by names and personages.
>Anxious to be noticed by " leading " persons.
>Blind follower. Discriminating respect.
>Knows how to follow wholesomely.

(51) *Sensitivity to ethical problems.*
>Frequently senses no ethical problem in situation.
>Evades ethical problem. Overscrupulous.
>Senses ethical problems readily.
>Keenly concerned over ethical problems.
>(Specify particular areas if important.)

(52) *Outstanding religious experience.*
>Has had no outstanding influential religious experience.
>Discovery of new insights and ideals.
>Reconstruction of intellectual ideas of religion.
>Drive to labor for some social cause.
>Prolonged struggle over some decision.
>Sudden access of new confidence and courage.

Definite resolve to live better life.

Notable conviction of sin, repentance and pardon.

(53) *Attitude toward Bible.*

Antagonistic. Reverences almost as fetish. Indifferent.

Chiefly concerned with critical questions.

Chiefly concerned with one type of content.

Intelligent reverence.

(Specify other attitudes if important.)

(54) *Personal devotions.*

Finds no meaning in private prayer.

Prays only with help of forms.

Prayer is routine with little real meaning.

Prayer and meditation hold important place in his life.

Prayer and fellowship with God hold central place in his experience.

(55) *Attitude toward public religious services led by others.*

Very critical. Absents himself frequently.

Routine attendant. Participates in good spirit.

Makes each an occasion of re-creation and new impetus.

(56) *Attitude toward the ministry.*

Regards ministry as opportunity to make money.

Regards ministry as opportunity for easy life.

Regards ministry as opportunity to " run " church organization.

Regards ministry as opportunity to become famous preacher.

Ready to serve without self-aggrandizement.

Tremendously and intelligently in earnest regardless of cost to self.

(57) *Interest in church's work.*

Uninterested. Slight interest.

Average interest.

More than usually interested. Absorbed.

(58) *Industriousness in church's work.*

Lazy. Just gets by. Average worker.

Good worker. Very hard worker.

(59) *His supreme love.*

Has he one? What is it?

(60) *His supreme purpose.*
> Has he one? What is it?

(61) *Stability of purpose.*
> Loses heart over failure. Head is turned by success.
> Shrinks from hardship and difficulty.
> Holds to purpose under most circumstances.
> Has held to main purpose a long while.
> Endures any hardship or difficulty cheerfully for sake of
> goal.

(62) *Influence of his religious life.*
> Harmful to others.
> Meddles in name of his faith.
> Uses stock phrases and sounds conventional.
> No influence one way or another.
> Stimulates helpful religious thought and practice.
> Instills enthusiasm for religious life.

(63) *Attitude toward his own call to the ministry.*
> Will probably decide not to go into ministry.
> Is now questioning his place in ministry.
> Has questioned it in seminary but becoming certain.
> Seems impelled by forces beyond himself.
> Overwhelming conviction which he accepts eagerly.

V. FINANCIAL RELATIONS

(64) *Spending.*
> Miserly. Spends beyond resources.
> Spends within resources.

(65) *Attitude toward financial obligations.*
> Known to be lax frequently in regard to obligations.
> Reported to be lax in financial obligations.
> Pays obligations promptly.
> Never in debt.

(66) *Attitude toward money he may receive.*
> Grasping. Indifferent. Wholesome.

(67) *Giving.*
> Usually excuses himself from contributing.
> Gives guardedly. Gives grudgingly.

Gives so as to imperil own financial resources.
Gives proportionately. Gives generously.
(68) *General estimate in financial relations.*
Very unsatisfactory. Questionable.
Satisfactory. Highly commendable.

If you have answered all these questions
carefully and conscientiously you will
know a great deal about yourself, and self-
knowledge is the beginning and the end
of wisdom. By this time you should
know with a great degree of certainty
whether or not the life of a minister is the
right life for you. One more question
remains to be considered — the relation
of the church to its minister. So to the
last chapter.

SUMMARY OF PERSONALITY ESTIMATION

(Place one check mark in the appropriate column after each section — I, II, etc.)

	Seems disqualified	Doubtful	Satisfactory	Very satisfactory	Out-standing
I. Physique and general appearance					
II. Mental and temperamental					
III. Social qualities					
IV. Religious life					
V. Financial relations					

Chapter Ten

THE CHURCH AND ITS MINISTER

HOW DO churches and ministers find each other? Is there an etiquette of ecclesiastical courtship, a technique by which the prospective minister gets linked up with his job? How does he make a change and relocate himself in a new field? And how does he know when to move? How can a church find the right minister and get rid of the wrong one? Is the same man equally a misfit in all places? Doesn't a minister run great peril in having to entrust his life to a cold-blooded ecclesiastical machine like a church? Or how can a church deal with its pastors humanely and justly and yet not be the victim of incompetence or senility?

Questions such as these indicate the importance of this chapter and its relevancy to any balanced consideration of the minister's life and work.

To begin with, much depends on the denominational type of organization. In episcopally governed churches the young minister goes where his bishop sends him, and moves when and where higher ecclesiastical authority (more or less influenced by a certain amount of judicious or injudicious political wirepulling) may direct. But in bodies with less dominant central authority the problem is not so simple. In churches like the Baptist, Congregational, Disciples and others with a democratic form of government both church and minister are supposed to be entirely free to call or to be called with no outward control, although there are, more often than some people think, searching and sincere prayers for divine guidance.

The traditional system in these churches is a procedure called " candidating." A pastorless church hears a succession of candidates for its pulpit, until the right man appears. Observation teaches however that often what determines the result is not so much the candidate's " rightness " as his superficial attractiveness, or sometimes the sheer weariness of a congregation exhausted by reviewing an endless line of major and minor prophets.

The evils of such a system are manifest. It is unfair to the candidate, who is often ill at ease when he tries to perform a sacred office under the critical gaze of a congregation appraising rather than sympathetic. Candidating also places a premium on the superficial and leaves undiscovered the deeper qualities of a prospective pastor. No man can be at his best while he is standing before a congregation and saying, in effect, " Here is how I look," and " Here is how I can pray," and " This is my number one go-getter sermon "! The man of sophistication and even of brass has the advantage in such a situation over a candidate with a modest soul and a publicity-shunning personality. How is it possible to judge on such evidence how well a man will wear, what reserves he has, what tact, insight, scholarship, moral courage, what self-effacing loyalty and devotion? And yet these qualities are certainly as essential in a good minister as a good voice, an attractive pulpit presence and one or two good sermons.

Obviously something needs to be done about this situation and one of the first steps is to change the church's method and the attitudes that lie behind it. Those attitudes are largely a hangover from the frontier days when the parson was called the preacher, and preaching, together with weddings, funerals and baptisms, was the major function of the ministry. Today the work of a minister is much more complicated and requires skills and resources not easily revealed by a trial sermon. Just glance over the earlier chapters of this book and ask yourself how much of what is there set forth can be discovered by a congregation listening to a string of candidates.

Here are some of the things a church needs to know about a prospective minister:

(1) *His personality.* Is he fair-minded, well poised, generous and kind? Has he a well ordered soul and a balanced outlook on life? Is he skillful in avoiding quarrels and yet courageous and firm in standing by basic Christian convictions? Can he be fair to those who disagree with him? Does he " go off half-cocked " or can he control his emotions and speak or act only with sound judgment and mature thought? Is he a wise counselor?

(2) *His habits.* Is he lazy or industrious? Is he neat and immaculate in dress and personal appearance, orderly of mind and in his affairs? Will he command the respect of the doctors, lawyers and businessmen of the community? How will women of culture, leaders in community life, regard him? What about his wife, his children and his home life?

(3) *His background and training.* What early home boyhood influences still manifest themselves? Where did he take his college work? Of what theological seminary is he a graduate? What degrees has he?

Are they really an index to his scholarly habits and ability?

(4) *His professional career.* What positions has he held? With what success? Why did he leave his last one or why does he want to leave it? Has he been popular while in the community? With whom and by reason of what qualities? Is he a builder who leaves a church stronger than he found it? How does he stand with men, with women, with youth, with children, with the outside community?

(5) *His ability as a minister.* Can he preach informing, uplifting sermons, imaginative, clear, inspiring? Is his preaching broad in its scope or is it all in one narrow groove? Has he any unpleasant mannerisms? Does he love people and make them his friends regardless of their wealth or social position? Can he organize and inspire his associates in the work of the church? Does he see the church in its relation to community and world problems? Is he loyal to his denomination but also to the church universal? Has he both a social and a personal message? Will his counsel and judgment be sought and increasingly respected the longer he lives in town? Above all, is he a man of God, with deep and genuine religious convictions, capable of making the church a sanctuary and its worship an experience of spiritual reality?

How is a church going to find out all these things? Obviously not just by reviewing a string of candidates. May I suggest, therefore, a better way which, in various forms, is coming into use among our stronger and wiser churches.

First of all, the church appoints a pastoral committee fairly representative of the congregation, making sure that it includes conservatives and progressives, the rich and the poor, the humble and the highbrow, men and women, adults and especially youth. This committee may then appoint a smaller executive committee to do the scouting. The executive committee goes out to seek a minister, knowing in advance what salary they can pay and what fixed requirements must be observed. It is to be hoped that age will not be one of these fixed requirements. It is both foolish and unfair for a committee to say that no man over a certain age will be considered. Chronological age has only a very faulty correlation with the qualities of real concern to the committee. Some men are more hopelessly set and unprogressive at thirty than others are at sixty. Remember the Boston boy who said, " My age chronologically is nine, sartorially only seven, psychologically nineteen, but esthetically, sociologically and epistemologically I am approaching one hundred! "

A pastoral committee is wise to be on its guard against candidates who nominate themselves or have evidently organized a campaign of endorsement among their friends. Some committees pass by such nominations and go out themselves to build up a list of ministers whom they know to be doing effective work. The names of such candidates will be given by members of the church, who know of them through friends and relatives; or by the state superintendent, who should always be consulted; or by various general denominational officials, who have opportunity to know available men and to see them in action. When the committee has accumulated a carefully selected list of promising men it can visit their churches anonymously, observe them under normal

workaday conditions, and make a choice based on a consideration of all the qualifications they have in mind. Of course
no man will fulfill all conditions one hundred per cent, but
the batting average will be higher than under the candidating system.

But, someone may object, this system benefits only the successful. What about the man who fails in his parish — how
is he ever to move? What about the man whose high Christian convictions on social matters or moral issues have made
him *persona non grata* to a hidebound conservative govern-
ing group in a timid, cowed or unawakened church or community?

The answer is that, if the minister is really a martyr and
not merely the victim of his own lack of grace and tact, his
friends will rally round him and find another field for him.
He may suffer financially but he will gain in every other way.
For, above all else, a minister must maintain his moral and
spiritual independence and self-respect. He ought not to
enter the ministry without recognizing that it may demand
martyrdom. At the same time no real martyr seeks to be one.
The wise minister builds up, in cash or in life insurance on
which he can borrow, a reserve sufficient to enable him to re-
sign at once, if the issue should be so acute as to make that
necessary, and still to subsist while seeking a new location.
But such situations are relatively rare. Most churches will
give a minister in conflict a reasonable time for readjustment.

For the man who has failed not because he is a martyr but
because he cannot measure up to the requirements of the job,
the situation is far more difficult. For him there are two
alternatives which may be picturesquely described as the

square-peg-in-a-round-hole solution and the drop-your-bucket-where-you-are solution.

The man who seems a failure in any given church may be simply a square peg in a round hole. He just is not adapted to that church or equipped to solve its problems, but he is a good sound man and should be transferred to a place where he will fit. Every denomination should have officials or placement committees to whom both churches and ministers can appeal for aid in such a problem.

On the other hand, the parson may wish to move just because of emotional restlessness. He has gone stale on the job, and will probably go stale on any other job he secures. His problem is mainly within himself. I once heard a psychiatrist say that Ralph Waldo Emerson decided to get away from himself by going to Naples. But when he arrived in Naples, there was Ralph Waldo Emerson!

The only solution for this condition is " drop your bucket where you are." Such a minister should preach every day as if a committee from some pastor-seeking church were in the congregation, but should plan his work and carry it on as if he expected to stay where he is for the next ten years. The man who feels he is stale on his job will be better off psychologically if he wins out where he is instead of running away. He needs a vacation, a summer school in a good seminary, a stimulating pastors' conference, a half dozen books thoroughly read and mastered to open up to him new vistas on preaching, church work and the lives of his people. Wherever there are human beings to work with, there a true minister will find an interesting job. If he really loves them and serves them with devoted understanding and sacrificial zeal he will be loved, honored and wanted. If he is loved, honored and wanted where he is, he will not lack opportunities to go elsewhere.

Nevertheless, there does come a time even in the happiest pastoral relations when a man should move. How can one know when that time comes? Failure of the church to meet its financial program or a falling off of attendance at services may serve as a barometer. If these conditions cannot be overcome the minister may well ask if he himself may not be the factor at fault and try to remove himself from the picture in order that the church may have the stimulus of new leadership and fresh ideas.

The time to move may also come with and because of success. A man's achievement in one field opens doors to larger opportunity. Should he accept a call to a larger church, a bigger job at an increased salary? The answer depends on the circumstances. How long has he been where he is? Has he really finished a chapter so that he can slip out as the leaves are turned? Or does the work he has been doing need his presence yet a while longer that it may " set," like concrete that has been poured but must have time to harden before the forms can safely be removed? No minister wants the work he has done to collapse the moment he leaves.

Then there are forward-looking criteria to be considered. What does the new opening offer in the way of adventure and new experience? Will it draw out and develop talents and interests largely unused as yet? Will it broaden the minister's outlook on life? Does it promise him a developing future or will he be expected to follow a treadmill of routine? Will he be glad he accepted it five years or ten years from now? What are the alternatives if he waits? Is he sure that the new people really want him and that it is a unanimous or at least a united call? My own personal principle has been to try to do my work where people wanted me and loved me, and nowhere else. It is a good recipe for a happy ministry. Better a smaller church and a less conspicuous position accompanied by love and loyalty than a more conspicuous and remunerative post at the price of contention, jealousy or indifference.

One part in the ordination program in some denominations is what is called the " charge to the people." An older and experienced minister, when a young man is ordained, gives some words of advice and counsel to the congregation on how to treat their minister. I attend many ordinations but have rarely been asked to take this part. So I propose to seize the opportunity to give it now and will close this chapter with a charge to the church concerning its care of a minister.

First of all I would remind the church that not only may a young minister's first church make or break him but almost any church may do so throughout his professional career. Ministers are far more influenced by the churches they have served than people ordinarily understand. Every pastor has tunes in him that are never played until the right church touches the keyboard.

The church's problem regarding its minister is how to develop him so as to bring out all his best qualities and utilize all his latent abilities. Of course it goes without saying that it will pay him a living salary, and pay it on time. An unpaid or inadequately paid minister is hardly in a position to render normal service. An old Cyprian proverb says, " A dog barks where he eats."

Next in importance is freedom. The minister must have

" liberty in prophesying " if he is to develop into a prophet. You, as one of the congregation, don't have to agree with all he says, but listen to it. You will hear few other men who try so hard to speak fairly, unselfishly and in accordance with the truth. You can be at least as generous as was Voltaire in the words attributed to him: " I disagree heartily with everything you have to say, but I will defend to the death your right to say it." Truth is much larger than any one man's version of it but it never grows by repression or fear. Go to your minister when you disagree with him and talk things over calmly and reasonably. Educate him if you can — give him facts he has overlooked and help restore forgotten emphases — but always in a spirit of reciprocity and openmindedness. Maybe you both can learn something, and truth will be the spark when flint is added unto steel.

Third, the church should be organized around both the minister's strength and his weakness. All men fill some parts of the minister's job better than others. The church should utilize to the utmost its pastor's strong points, and where he is weak organize to compensate for that weakness. For example, it may be discovered that the pastor has a flair for preaching but is a poor businessman and lets the leaks in the roof go unrepaired and the leaks in the church's financial policy go undiscovered. What then? The church should capitalize on his preaching ability by forming a strong publicity committee to back it, and then proceed to organize the business affairs so that leaks both aquatic and financial will be repaired without his ever knowing about them.

The next responsibility of the church toward its minister is to expand his horizons. He should have a fund for books — and time to read them. He should travel. No church is

14705

justified in begrudging its minister a good vacation. He will be working for it every minute by gaining new ideas and fresh outlooks on life. Personally I deeply regret that I never had a chance to visit Palestine until I was fifty years of age. I realize now how much richer my understanding of the Bible and consequently my preaching would have been could I have gone to the Holy Land at thirty. The church that can catch a hopeful young parson and send him to Egypt, Greece and Palestine early in his career should do it by all means. Incidentally, he will see New York, England, France, Switzerland, and Italy en route.

Is there anything more a church can do for its minister? Yes, one very important thing which can be stated very briefly: It can make his wife happy. Just a little concern for the upkeep of the parsonage, a new coat of paint, some up-to-date plumbing and an additional room for the new baby may make all the difference in the world. I don't mean that either the minister or his wife should have what Dean Gilkey calls "the prima donna attitude." They should have work enough so that they will not behave like spoiled children. But a church that loves the pastor and his wife, and shows it, will contribute a very important part in the task of training ministers for a world which so desperately needs strong, courageous, Christlike spiritual leaders.

———

As you have read these reflections and counsels of one who has spent many happy and, he hopes, fruitful years in the service of his fellow men under the aegis of the church, have you felt an affirmative response? Have you heard the summons to such service more clearly, with both heart and mind? The life of the minister is no bed of roses. His task is exacting and demands complete dedication. Mere enthusiasm, mere desire to serve, is not sufficient. Neither the head alone nor the heart alone can guide the minister; emotion and reason must consent to each other, must be wedded into an integrated whole whose center is God. Perhaps as you have read you have felt doubtful. The requirements seemed too great, the sacrifices too hard. If your doubts will not down, it may be that you should seek another kind of life. But it is to be remembered that every sincere man has moments of uncertainty, when he feels that he is not equal to his task, that his efforts benefit neither himself nor anyone else, and that the servant of God and God's church, because his aims are so high, may seem to fall further short of them than does the man who pursues objectives more tangible and mundane. My final advice is this: Make your decision in the light of reason, but of the highest reason. I hope it will be an affirmative decision. If it is, you will be singularly fortunate among men, for the work that lies before you offers rewards greater and more enduring than all the world's treasures. And so — God speed you!